Decisive Essays
On
AI And Law

Advanced Series On
Artificial Intelligence (AI)
And Law

Dr. Lance B. Eliot, MBA, PhD

Disclaimer: This book is presented solely for educational and entertainment purposes. The author and publisher are not offering it as legal, accounting, or other professional services advice. The author and publisher make no representations or warranties of any kind and assume no liabilities of any kind with respect to the accuracy or completeness of the contents and specifically disclaim any implied warranties of merchantability or fitness of use for a particular purpose. Neither the author nor the publisher shall be held liable or responsible to any person or entity with respect to any loss or incidental or consequential damages caused, or alleged to have been caused, directly or indirectly, by the information or programs contained herein. Every company is different and the advice and strategies contained herein may not be suitable for your situation.

DEDICATION

To my incredible daughter, Lauren, and my incredible son, Michael.

Forest fortuna adiuvat (from the Latin; good fortune favors the brave).

CONTENTS

Note: Visuals are collected together in Appendix B, rather than being interjected into the chapter contents, for ease of reading, enhanced flow, and to see the visuals altogether.

ACKNOWLEDGMENTS

I have been the beneficiary of advice and counsel by many friends, colleagues, family, investors, and many others. I want to thank everyone that has aided me throughout my career. I write from the heart and the head, having experienced first-hand what it means to have others around you that support you during the good times and the tough times.

To renowned scholar and colleague, Dr. Warren Bennis, I offer my deepest thanks and appreciation, especially for his calm and insightful wisdom and support.

To billionaire and university trustee, Mark Stevens and his generous efforts toward funding and supporting the Stevens Center for Innovation.

To Peter Drucker, William Wang, Aaron Levie, Peter Kim, Jon Kraft, Cindy Crawford, Jenny Ming, Steve Milligan, Chis Underwood, Frank Gehry, Buzz Aldrin, Steve Forbes, Bill Thompson, Dave Dillon, Alan Fuerstman, Larry Ellison, Jim Sinegal, John Sperling, Mark Stevenson, Anand Nallathambi, Thomas Barrack, Jr., and many other innovators and leaders that I have met and gained mightily from doing so.

Thanks to Ed Trainor, Kevin Anderson, James Hickey, Wendell Jones, Ken Harris, DuWayne Peterson, Mike Brown, Jim Thornton, Abhi Beniwal, Al Biland, John Nomura, Eliot Weinman, John Desmond, and many others for their unwavering support during my career.

Thanks goes to the Stanford University CodeX Center for Legal Informatics and the Stanford University Computer Science department for their generous support, and for the insightful and inspirational discussions and feedback from my many fellow colleagues there.

And most of all thanks as always to Lauren and Michael, for their ongoing support and for having seen me writing and heard much of this material during the many months involved in writing it. To their patience and willingness to listen.

Dr. Lance B. Eliot

CHAPTER 1

INTRODUCTION TO
AI AND LAW

This book provides a series of crucial essays encompassing the burgeoning field of AI and the law.

These essays are ostensibly standalone and do not require any prior familiarity with the AI and law topic. You are welcome to read the essays in whichever order you might prefer. The essays have been numbered and sequenced as chapters for ease of referring to the discussions and not due to any need to read one before another.

The essays provide a helpful overview and entry point into the field of AI and law. You will find the essays relatively easy to read and eschew arcane techno-terminology, aiming to layout the vital aspects in clear language and seeking to be readily grasped. The chosen topics entail the latest and hottest trends in the AI and law arena.

For those of you that are potentially interested in knowing more about AI and the law in a deeper way, you might consider my two other books on this subject:

- *"AI and Legal Reasoning Essentials"* by Dr. Lance Eliot
- *"Artificial Intelligence and LegalTech Essentials"* by Dr. Lance Eliot

Those are more akin to textbook-style orientations to the AI and the law field. Both books are available on Amazon and at major bookseller sites. The first book listed provides a comprehensive and detailed exploration of AI and law, while the second book tends to focus primarily on LegalTech and the blending of AI.

One of the most frequent questions that I get asked during my webinars, seminars, and college courses about AI and the law consists of what the phrase "AI and the law" actually refers to.

That's a fair question and deserves a useful answer. In a moment, I will borrow from my other books to provide an explanation about the meaning of "AI and the law" and then dovetail into a brief indication about each of the essays contained in this collection.

Per the essays, you'll end up seeing that there is a great deal of enthusiastic spirit for AI and the law, and likewise a sizable dollop of angst and trepidation about the intertwining of the two. In my view, whether you love it or hate it, there is no stopping the steamroller moving ahead that is going to infuse AI together with the law.

I would urge that any lawyer worth their salt ought to be learning about AI and the law. This will assuredly be especially important for those that are just now starting their legal careers, which I mention because the odds are that the convergence of AI and the law will have an especially pronounced effect throughout your lifelong legal efforts.

For those of you that might be going a more so academic route in the legal realm, rather than being a practitioner of the law per se, the beauty of AI and the law is that there is ample room for new research and a grand opportunity to make a demonstrative mark on the field.

Despite the fact that the field of AI and the law has been studied for many years, dating back to the beginning of the AI field itself, please be aware that we have only scratched the surface on this interweaving. Anyone with a desire to push the boundaries of these two realms will readily find plenty of rampways to do so.

If you are curious about the possible research avenues to pursue, make sure to take a look at my book on *AI and Legal Reasoning Essentials* since it provides a solid foundation on the research to-date and postulates what might be coming down the pike in future research activities. I bid you welcome to the field and wish you the best of luck in your endeavors.

AI And Law

In my viewpoint, Artificial Intelligence (AI) and the field of law are synergistic partners. The intertwining of AI and Law can generally be categorized into two major approaches:

- **AI as applied to Law**
- **Law as applied to AI**

Let us consider each of those two approaches.

AI As Applied To Law

AI as applied to law consists of trying to utilize AI technologies and AI techniques for the embodiment of law, potentially being able to perform legal tasks and undertake legal reasoning associated with the practice of law. Those scholars, experts, and practitioners that have this focus are using AI to aid or integrate artificial intelligence into how humans practice law, either augmenting lawyers and other legal professionals or possibly replacing them in the performance of various legal tasks.

Crafting such AI is especially hard to accomplish, problematic in many ways, and there have been and continue to emerge a myriad of attempts to achieve this difficult goal or aspiration. The rise of LegalTech and LawTech, which is modern digital technology used to support and enable lawyers, law offices, and the like throughout the practice of law are gradually and inexorably being bolstered by the addition of AI capabilities.

There are many indications already of this trend rapidly expanding in the existing and growing LegalTech and LawTech marketplace. Notably, the potent AI and LegalTech/LawTech combination has been drawing the rapt attention of Venture Capitalists (VCs). According to figures by the National Venture Capital Association (NVCA), the last several years have witnessed VC's making key investments of over one billion dollars towards law-related tech startups, many of which have some form of an AI capability involved.

Most of the AI developed so far for LegalTech and LawTech is only able to assist lawyers and legal professions in rather modest and simplistic ways. For example, AI might speed-up the search for documents during e-discovery or might enhance the preparation of a contract by identifying pertinent contractual language from a corpus of prior contracts.

Where the field of applying AI to law is seeking to head involves having AI that can perform legal minded tasks that human lawyers and other legal professionals perform. In essence, creating AI systems that can undertake legal reasoning. This is commonly referred to as AI for Legal Reasoning (AILR).

In a sense, legal reasoning goes to the core of performing legal tasks and is considered the ultimate pinnacle as it were for the efforts to try and apply AI to law. It is undoubtedly one of the most exciting areas of the AI-applied-to-law arena and one that holds both tremendous promise and perhaps some angst and possible somber qualms.

Law As Applied To AI

The other major approach that combines AI and law focuses on the law as applied AI. This is an equally crucial perspective on the AI and law topic.

Sometimes this is also referred to as the **Governance of AI**, though there are those that believe that to be a somewhat narrower perspective on the topic. In any case, the focus is primarily on the governance of AI and how our laws might need to be revised, updated, or revamped in light of AI systems.

You likely already know that AI is experiencing quite a resurgence and has become a key focus of the tech field, along with gaining attention throughout society. AI is being rapidly infused into a wide variety of industries and domain specialties, including AI in the financial sector, AI in the medical domain, and so on.

This rapid pace of AI adoption has opened the eyes of society about the benefits of AI but also has gradually brought to the forefront many of the costs or negative aspects that AI can bring forth. Some assert that our existing laws are insufficient to cope with the advances that AI is producing.

Thus, the need to closely examine our existing laws and possibly revamp them for an era and future of ubiquitous AI.

Expected Impacts

Let's consider how AI and the law can impact those in the AI field, and also contemplate how it can impact those in the field of law.

If you are an AI specialist, you should certainly be interested in the AI and law topic, either due to the possibilities of advancing AI by discovering how to leverage AI into the legal domain or due to the potential of how existing and future laws are going to impact the exploration and fielding of AI systems.

If you are a lawyer or legal specialist, you ought to be interested in the AI and law topic too, for the same reasons as the AI specialist, though perhaps with some added stake in the game.

What is the added stake?

If AI can ultimately become advanced enough to practice law, there is concern by some that it could potentially replace the need for human lawyers and other human legal-related law practitioners.

Some liken this to the famous and telling remark about commitment as exhibited via a chicken and a pig. A chicken and a pig are walking along and discussing what they might do together, and the chicken offers that perhaps they ought to open a restaurant that serves ham-n-eggs. Upon a moment of reflection, the pig speaks up and says that if they did so, the chicken would only be involved (making the eggs), while the pig would end-up being fully committed (being the bacon).

In that sense, AI specialists in this topic are involved, while legal specialists and lawyers are committed.

Meanwhile, for those of you squarely in the field of law, lest you think that AI specialists are to be spared the same fate of being overtaken by AI, you will be perhaps surprised to know that there are efforts underway to craft AI that makes AI, such as in the field of Machine Learning (ML), a specialty known as AutoML, which could potentially put human developers of AI out of a job.

What is good for the goose is good for the gander. Or, it might be that what is bad for the goose is equally bad for the gander.

About These Essays

Now that you've gotten an initial synopsis regarding the topic of AI and law, let's take a moment to briefly take a look at the essays assembled for this decisive collection.

Chapter 1 – Introduction To AI And Law

Key briefing points about this chapter:

- This book is a collection of crucial essays about AI and the law

- The essays are provided as numbered chapters (the sequence is not essential)

- AI and the law consist of two key facets

- One facet is AI as applied to the law (a mainstay of this collection)

- The other facet is applying the law to AI (i.e., governance of AI)

Chapter 2 - AI & Law: Autonomous Legal Reasoning

Key briefing points about this chapter:

- A misleading media portrayal about AI is that all AI is presumptively the same (it is not)

- There are various Levels of Autonomy (LoA) associated with AI, proffering increasing capacities

- A new approach to LoA for AI-based Legal Reasoning systems has been gaining attention

- AI Legal Reasoning (AILR) is ranked into seven distinct categories of autonomous capability

- This provides a handy means to compare AI & Law products and LegalTech offerings

Chapter 3 - AI & Law: Robo-Lawyer Hyperbole

Key briefing points about this chapter:

- The "robo-lawyer" phrase is pervasive and a stand-in for robot-like AI Legal Reasoning

- Unfortunately, the phraseology tends to be mainly hyperbole and overinflates expectations

- It will be hard to mitigate the catchphrase since it has innate stickiness and a flavorful allure

- One proposed replacement would be to instead refer to levels of autonomy of AI in the law

- Akin to levels associated with self-driving cars, the new phrasing is catchy too and more apt

Chapter 4 - AI & Law: Legal Singularity

Key briefing points about this chapter:

- A notable theory in AI is that someday there will be *The Singularity* (i.e., AI becomes sentient)

- No one can say for sure that this crossover into sentience will happen, nor when it might

- Some assert that the field of law will have its own AI moment known as the Legal Singularity

- It is useful to consider the ramifications of Legal Singularity to the law, the legal profession, etc.

- A leading and controversial hypothesis is that the law would no longer have any uncertainty

Chapter 5 - AI & Law: Legal Micro-Directives

Key briefing points about this chapter:

- Legal scholars have proposed that we might inevitably make use of legal micro-directives

- A legal micro-directive is a legal rule that goes beyond today's limited paper-based realm

- Envision a legal rule that is computer-based and able to be made available when needed

- Also, ramp-up the computer-enablement by adding Artificial Intelligence (AI) into the mix

- This bodes for an era in which the law is smartly conveyed in real-time and decidedly on-point

Chapter 6 - AI & Law: Legal Argumentation

Key briefing points about this chapter:

- One might boldly suggest that humans are essentially biologically-based arguing machines

- Besides our general propensity to argue, argumentation in the law is a paramount skill

- Artificial Intelligence (AI) is going to increasingly be utilized for legal argumentation purposes

- There are four primary ways that AI-enabled legal reasoning will be used in argumentation

- The gradual expansion of AI in the law will serve to powerfully enhance legal argumentation

Chapter 7 - AI & Law: Principles Of Justice

Key briefing points about this chapter:

- Artificial Intelligence (AI) will undoubtedly continue to be integrated into the practice of law

- Some suggest this will undercut a semblance of justice, while others say it will bolster justice

- A sensible place to start such a discussion involves defining *justice* (using key precepts)

- AI legal reasoning systems can apply to each of the defined seven principles of justice

- Ascertaining the ultimate outcome of applying AI will be up to how we choose to proceed

Chapter 8 - AI & Law: Reengineering The Law

Key briefing points about this chapter:

- An oft saying in the tech field is that you should stridently avoid paving the cow paths
- This catchy phrase asserts that you must do reengineering before adopting new technologies
- This matters because many of today's legal ways in the courts and in law firms are outmoded
- Meanwhile, new tech such as AI is merely being plunked on top of those "as is" processes
- Hoped-for gains and value from AI-based LegalTech must be accompanied by reengineering

Chapter 9 – AI & Law: Legal Sentimentality

Key briefing points about this chapter:

- Questions abound about the role of sentimentality and emotion with the halls of justice
- A famous court case entailing a *Tribute to a Dog* is legendary for a sentimental closing argument
- AI can be utilized to try and gauge sentimentality within a written record of a court case
- There is also the use of AI for real-time sentimentality detection and for opinion mining
- The future could entail using AI routinely in this rooting out the role, but qualms remain

Chapter 10 - AI & Law: Three Tiers Of The Law

Key briefing points about this chapter:

- Currently, the practice of law is tightly controlled and there is essentially just one tier

- Some argue that we need a second tier consisting of non-lawyers certified to also do the law

- Acrimonious debates covering the benefits versus risks of a two-tiered approach are plentiful

- Coming down the road will be the potential of a third-tier consisting of Artificial Intelligence (AI)

- Questions abound about the tiers and the (shocking) chance of collapsing back into one tier

Chapter 11 - AI & Law: Turing Test

Key briefing points about this chapter:

- There isn't any AI yet today that is sentient and nor reaches the level of full human intelligence

- Nonetheless, there might someday be such vaunted AI and we'll need to know that it exists

- Within the AI field, there is a type of famous test for this known as the Turing Test

- It makes sense to recast the Turing Test into the field of law as it relates to AI and the law

- Once there is AI-enabled autonomous legal reasoning we'll want to validate its capabilities

Chapter 12 - AI & Law: Next Era Of Law

Key briefing points about this chapter:

- American history and American law are joined at the hip and are worth jointly studying

- Legal scholars suggest that there have been three major eras of the law in the U.S.

- The three eras are known as (1) Age of discovery, (2) Age of faith, and (3) Age of Anxiety

- Questions arise as to what the next and thus fourth era will be

- Among the hypothesized next eras is the possibility of AI in the law as a key ingredient

Chapter 13 – AI & Law: Pure Logic Insufficiency

Key briefing points about this chapter:

- Some believe that we ought to be able to turn the law into a set of axiomatic logic

- Doing so would presumably make the law easily computerized and become widely accessible

- Logic-based law could theoretically enable computational legality determinations

- Ongoing attempts at using AI in this quest for a pure logic approach are underway

- Complexity ensues and there are pitfalls aplenty that still are to be resolved

Chapter 14 – AI & Law: Legal Simplification

Key briefing points about this chapter:

- An ongoing drumbeat is whether the laws are overly convoluted and need to be simplified

- Simplifying the laws might provide upsized benefits for the public and the practice of law

- Not everyone is convinced that law simplification is an answer and might worsen matters

- AI has the potential for providing a type of legal simplification engine

- There are qualms that the AI simplifying machinations could bode for legal difficulties

Chapter 15 - AI & Law: Dualism With Morality

Key briefing points about this chapter:

- The law has a close cousin, morality, for which there is at times agreement and sometimes not

- Society has wrestled with the dualism of the law and morality for millennia

- Recent advances in AI have led to attempts at embedding AI-enabled moral agents into software

- Likewise, there is a need to embed AI-enabled law-oriented agents into software

- Inevitably these two types of AI agencies will clash and the question of resolution is still open

Chapter 16 – AI & Law: Legal Definitions of AI

Key briefing points about this chapter:

- Definitions are the lifeblood of the law and inextricably the practice of law too

- Many a court case has hinged precariously on the definition of this word or that phrase

- Meanwhile, consider that AI is gradually and inexorably coming into the field of law

- And yet there is ample ambiguity about what "AI" entails and definitions of AI are aplenty

- This gives rise to examining a definition of AI as codified into the National Defense Act

Chapter 17 - AI & Law: Growth In Laws

Key briefing points about this chapter:

- A recent study estimated how many laws there are today and growth rates over time

- The research results offer vital food-for-thought about the future of the law

- Thinking outside-the-box, ponder the number of lawyers in a past, present, and future sense

- An additional twist for the future will be the advent of AI-enabled legal reasoning systems

- Advances in AI and the law might impact the number of laws and the number of lawyers

Chapter 18 - AI & Law: Legal Deserts

Key briefing points about this chapter:

- A rising consideration in the legal profession has to do with qualms about legal deserts

- Legal deserts are geographic areas that have a dearth of available attorneys

- The public in legal deserts are potentially unable or unaware of exercising their rights

- The advent of remote access and the lure of local opportunities might aid in this matter

- In addition, the increasing use of Artificial Intelligence (AI) can play a significant role

Chapter 19 - AI & Law: Open Records

Key briefing points about this chapter:

- There are strident calls for greater open access to court records

- Doing so will provide vital data needed for holistic policy analyses of justice

- Another important use would aid in bolstering the advent of AI in the law

- AI that utilizes Machine Learning requires extensive data to be suitably trained

- Via plentiful access to court data the efforts to devise AI Legal Reasoning would be aided

Chapter 20 - AI & Law: About OpenAI's GPT-3

Key briefing points about this chapter:

- GPT-3 is an AI-based software tool proffered by the for-profit firm OpenAI

- Acts like a souped-up "autocomplete" taking seed text and producing output text

- Was computationally trained via scrapping data across the Internet

- Legal profession applicability such as able to auto-generate contracts

- Potential legal liability issues regarding auto-generating medical advice, etc.

Chapter 21 - AI & Law: Legal Judgment Prediction

Key briefing points about this chapter:

- Lawyers are continually having to try and predict what will happen in a legal case

- Legal Judgment Prediction (LJP) involves devising computer models for making such predictions

- The use of Artificial Intelligence (AI) is aiming to boost the predictive capabilities of LJP

- There are advantages and also downsides to using AI-powered LJP predictions

- If AI LJP becomes superbly predictive it could have a dramatic judicial impact

Chapter 22 – AI & Law: Legal Doctrines

Key briefing points about this chapter:

- The law consists of numerous and vital doctrines that are invented rules-of-law

- One well-known instance was first derived via a court case of the wagon and the donkey

- AI is anticipated to gradually and inexorably become adept at AI-based legal reasoning

- An unresolved question entails how such AI systems will be imbued with law doctrines

- By exploring the doctrine rising the wagon and donkey we can gauge Machine Learning (ML)

Chapter 23 - AI & Law: Tech-Hype Curves

Key briefing points about this chapter:

- Tech-Hype curves showcase which tech is being over-hyped and which tech is settling in

- Each year the Gartner Group releases iterations of their famous Tech-Hype curves

- Recent AI & Law advances were categorized by Gartner's latest LegalTech hype curve

- Upcoming are legal chatbots, third-party risk management, AI in legal practices, etc.

- But some AI & Law tech efforts are predicted as doomed, others are on verge of a reboot

Chapter 24 - AI & Law: LegalTech Startups

Key briefing points about this chapter:

- Many attorneys harbor a dream to do a startup business based on a LegalTech idea they have

- An entrepreneurial-minded lawyer needs to think ahead and prepare for the rough journey

- The good news is that the VC/PE funding for LegalTech startups still seems to be doing well

- The "bad news" is that there are lots of LegalTech flops and failures, so be forewarned

- Abide by the included list of 20 key factors for your startup and you'll have a better chance

Chapter 25 - AI & Law: LegalTech Product Ideas

Key briefing points about this article:

- This is a continuation of an earlier article about the twenty key factors for a LegalTech startup

- In this piece, the focus is on two of the foundational factors: (1) the problem, (2) the solution

- If a LegalTech founder cannot clearly state the problem and proposed solution things will falter

- An example used herein discusses a startup proposing a contract life cycle management system

- Use these insights to ensure that your LegalTech startup has sharply devised its vision

More About This Book

For anyone opting to use this book in a class or course that pertains to these topics, note that Appendix A contains suggestions about how to use the book in a classroom setting.

Furthermore, Appendix B contains a set of slides that depict many of the salient points made throughout the book.

In some of my prior books, I've interspersed the slides into the chapter contents, but feedback by readers has generally been that readers prefer to not have the textual flow become disrupted by the slides, and instead prefer to have the supplemental material assembled altogether into an appendix.

To make sure that you are aware of those added materials, you'll notice that the ending of each chapter provides a quick reminder about the visual depictions that are available in Appendix B.

And so, with this overall orientation to the nature and structure of this book in mind, please proceed to read the essays and learn about the field of AI and law. I'm truly hoping that you'll find the essays mentally engaging and stimulative to the nature of how the law is being practiced and what the future of the law might become.

Note: *For supplemental materials depicting the aspects discussed in this chapter, refer to Appendix B, which contains various augmented diagrams, charts, and additional related facets of relevance.*

CHAPTER 2

AI & LAW: AUTONOMOUS LEGAL REASONING

Key briefing points about this essay:

- A misleading media portrayal about AI is that all AI is presumptively the same (it is not)

- There are various Levels of Autonomy (LoA) associated with AI, proffering increasing capacities

- A new approach to LoA for AI-based Legal Reasoning systems has been gaining attention

- AI Legal Reasoning (AILR) is ranked into seven distinct categories of autonomous capability

- This provides a handy means to compare AI & Law products and LegalTech offerings

Introduction

AI is increasingly being applied to the field of law and the legal industry, including that many LegalTech providers are inexorably augmenting their wares via advances in Machine Learning (ML) and Natural Language Processing (NLP).

Unfortunately, it is difficult for legal professionals to readily discern what value these AI improvements add. The vendors are apt to either overstate the capabilities of the AI-empowerment or proffer outsized and outrageous marketing absurdity that suggests the tech has miraculously become a vaunted "robo-lawyer" (implying a semblance of sentience or outstretched superhuman abilities).

One of the principal reasons that this confounding state of affairs exists is due to the noteworthy lack of a convenient and readily usable way to measure or gauge the degree of AI being infused into these emerging state-of-the-art LegalTech offerings.

As astutely generally opined by the famous management guru Dr. Peter Drucker, you can't manage that which you can't or don't measure.

In short, there is no existing standard that depicts the range of levels of how AI can be applied to the law and thus leaves open a gap or omission in sizing up computer-based systems within the legal industry. It would indubitably be helpful and immensely prudent for stakeholders in the legal realm to consider establishing a reasoned set of measures that could be utilized and serve as a rationalizing approach to conveying the extent that AI is being employed.

Analogous Case Of Self-Driving Cars

Shifting gears, we can consider how other domains have dealt with a similar conundrum.

Consider the case of AI-enabled Autonomous Vehicles (AV).

There is a widely known worldwide standard for self-driving cars that have been successfully promulgated by the globally recognized SAE standards group. You might be vaguely aware of the standard and its various stated levels of autonomy.

For example, existing Tesla's using their Autopilot software are considered to be semi-autonomous and rated as a Level 2 on the official SAE scale that ranges from zero to five. At Level 2, the vehicle requires that a human driver must be present and attentive at all times for the driving task. The AI is considered an Advanced Driver-Assistance System (ADAS), merely assisting the human, and is decidedly not operating at a truly autonomous level of functionality.

Waymo is known for its pursuit of Level 4 self-driving cars. Per the SAE standard, a Level 4 is rated as an autonomous vehicle, meaning that there is no need for a human driver and no expectation that a human driver is at the wheel. Level 4 is somewhat restrictive in that the AI driving system is allowed to only be able to drive in particular settings, such as able to drive exclusively in sunny weather or specific geography of a defined geo-boxed area.

The topmost level of autonomy is stipulated as Level 5, which exceeds the capabilities of Level 4 by stipulating that the AI that must be able to drive in essentially any circumstance that a human driver would potentially be able to drive a car, thus removing the restrictions associated with Level 4.

The advantage of such a taxonomy is that it is relatively easy to compare various brands of self-driving cars, merely by indicating the level that each has attained. Furthermore, this is a succinct way to communicate about autonomy and consists of simply stating the level number achieved.

That's what is likewise needed in the arena of applying AI to the law.

To wit, another famous idiom that pertains here is to try to avoid reinventing the wheel, as it were, and we might as well reuse that which already works well elsewhere. Let's marry together the facets of AI autonomy as used in self-driving cars to the need for a set of autonomy levels for the field of AI as applied to law, doing so with a mindful realization to adjust and transform those AI autonomous principles into ones that are directly fitting to the AI and law domain.

The Seven Levels Of AI Legal Reasoning

Based on the latest research, there are seven levels of autonomy that can be used to appropriately designate the application of automation and AI as it applies to legal discourse and reasoning:

- Level 0: No legal automation

- Level 1: Simple Automation for legal assistance

- Level 2: Advanced Automation for legal assistance

- Level 3: Semi-Autonomous Automation for legal assistance

- Level 4: Domain Autonomous legal advisor

- Level 5: Fully Autonomous legal advisor

- Level 6: Superhuman Autonomous legal advisor

Briefly, the levels range from 0 to 6, establishing that the least amount of legal AI automation is designated as zero and the topmost would be a six. This numbering is easy to remember and provides a comprehensive range to encompass all facets of AI embellishment.

Most of today's LegalTech would rate as a Level 1, and for those that have extended their software with some amount of bona fide AI add-ons they would possibly rate as a Level 2.

Level 3 consists of semi-autonomous automation that provides legal assistance, which today is mainly done on a pilot or experimental basis and represents the cusp over which the next step lands incrementally into the actual autonomous territory or designated as Level 4. At Level 4, the AI autonomy is considered restrictive and pertains to a subdomain of law, while at Level 5 the AI is considered fully capable across all avenues of the law.

There is also a futuristic Level 6, providing a level for the possibility, though presumably remote, that the AI could someday eclipse human intelligence and become so-called super-human.

In contrast, the SAE self-driving car standard tops out at the human driving capability and does not portend that one day it might be feasible for cars to be driven by the AI in a manner beyond that of human drivers (this is a matter that some critics say should be added to the SAE standard).

Conclusion

Overall, the notion presented here is that by thoughtfully applying an already accepted convention of AI autonomy, yet judiciously transforming it to the needs of AI as applied to law, we can reduce the exaggerated claims and other unruly chatter about AI in the legal industry.

Note: *For supplemental materials depicting the aspects discussed in this chapter, refer to Appendix B, which contains various augmented diagrams, charts, and additional related facets of relevance*

CHAPTER 3
AI & LAW:
ROBO-LAWYER
HYPERBOLE

Key briefing points about this essay:

- The "robo-lawyer" phrase is pervasive and a stand-in for robot-like AI Legal Reasoning

- Unfortunately, the phraseology tends to be mainly hyperbole and overinflates expectations

- It will be hard to mitigate the catchphrase since it has innate stickiness and a flavorful allure

- One proposed replacement would be to instead refer to levels of autonomy of AI in the law

- Akin to levels associated with self-driving cars, the new phrasing is catchy too and more apt

Introduction

A particular phrase can become pervasive and have an abundance of stickiness, despite limitations or paucity in everyday practical terms of the merits entailed in the wording. If the phraseology happens to be catchy, it will tend to catch on.

Furthermore, when a vacuum exists such that there is nothing else as alluring to fill the void, you can bet your bottom dollar that the otherwise questionable catchphrase will prevail. The odds are that it will take on a life of its own, being bandied about and used time and time again, gaining added traction as it merrily rolls along.

Want a tangible example of this somewhat abstract precept?

A notably prime example would be the nebulous and now disconcertingly infamous reference to "robo-lawyer," also stated less poetically as a *robot lawyer*.

A glance online provides voluminous indications of articles and postings that relish using the robo-lawyer moniker as a headline-grabbing stunt. Admittedly, the usage tends to work and gets the attention of readers. In that sense, it is an effective trigger or communicative signal.

Plus, one might argue that there is nothing else that so succinctly conveys the same notion, namely the idea that Artificial Intelligence (AI) is gradually entering into the legal domain and increasingly becoming part-and-parcel of the latest LegalTech offerings.

Unfortunately, the robo-lawyer notion carries a lot of baggage with it.

The innate implication of the vaunted phrase is that there exist instances of AI that are sentient or that have reached a level of capability equal to human intelligence.

Lawyers and other legal professionals become instinctively worried that they are on the verge of being replaced by such AI.

The public-at-large is led to believe that a legal chatbot can provide comparable legal advice as would a human lawyer.

And so on.

Let's be clear about this and please know that there is no such AI today that can analyze the law and proffer legal advice in anything akin to that of a flesh-and-blood attorney. Sure, AI can demonstrably aid a lawyer by piecing together contract passages when drafting a new contract or conduct a quick search across a corpus of court cases to find ones that are salient and notable for a new case being pursued, but none of this is the same as exhibiting the robust and cognitive prowess embodied in humanoid lawyering expertise.

Over time, the AI is getting better and being improved by advances in Natural Language Processing (NLP), Machine Learning (ML), Knowledge-Based Systems (KBS), and so on, though the possibility of sentience is a farfetched dream and likewise so is the use of an AI-based robot lawyer that autonomously dispenses bona fide legal advice.

For now, we need to keep a balanced perspective that AI does have merit, and will additively boost those that practice law, and yet realize too that AI has a long way to go before it gains substantive autonomy. In the meantime, what shall we do about the handy robo-lawyer naming that regrettably overstates and misleads in both tone and substance? A sounder approach consists of referring to levels of autonomy and as specifically geared toward the field of AI and law.

As mentioned in Chapter 2, there are seven levels of autonomy that can be used to appropriately designate the application of automation and AI as it applies to legal discourse and reasoning:

Level 0: No legal automation

Level 1: Simple Automation for legal assistance

Level 2: Advanced Automation for legal assistance

Level 3: Semi-Autonomous Automation for legal assistance

Level 4: Domain Autonomous legal advisor

Level 5: Fully Autonomous legal advisor

Level 6: Superhuman Autonomous legal advisor

Those of you familiar with self-driving cars are likely aware that a worldwide standard exists for referring to levels of autonomy in the case of cars, trucks, and other ground-based vehicles, and uses a similar format or convention to depict the various levels of autonomy.

Having such a systematic means to refer to self-driving is handy since it can readily denote whether a given AI-based driving system is merely aiding a human driver or intended to replace a human driver. This also allows for catching those that seem to exaggerate or stretch what they offer as an AI driver by asking them which level of autonomy their vehicle has actually achieved.

We can do the same in the field of law.

For example, a new feature added into an e-discovery software package might make use of NLP, allowing for queries to be made by using everyday conversational language rather than having to use an arcane and highly tech-oriented set of commands.

Is this added capability of NLP able to unabashedly be touted as a robo-lawyer?

A vendor might certainly hope so, and due to there not being any particular restriction or global definition regarding the meaning of robo-lawyer, this kind of grandstanding can easily be undertaken.

If the NLP were to be compared to the levels of AI and law autonomy, presumably it would come into the Level 2 category, in which case, we would all immediately know that the NLP has not leaped into the autonomous realm as yet.

After a while, once the levels become familiar and commonly referenced, the succinctness of referring to level numbers would be quickly recognized, just as is the case for those in the self-driving arena. Existing Tesla's using Autopilot is known to be at Level 2, while Waymo and it's self-driving public tryouts consist of Level 4 vehicles. Autopilot is still at the driver assistance stages, while Waymo is piloting at the autonomous no-driver-needed levels.

At first, it will be hard to promulgate the autonomous levels of AI and law and relinquish the flashier robo-lawyer convention. Gradually and inexorably, it will become apparent that all parties should have an alternative means to realistically establish where AI stands in terms of performing legal reasoning and do so with the quickness of stating what level of autonomy a LegalTech system or piece of software has attained.

Conclusion

It is time to drop the robo-lawyer hyperbolic references and embrace a prudent and reasonably crisp set of levels for fairly stating what AI is legitimately contributing to the field of law.

Admittedly, doing so has quite an uphill battle since there is nothing seemingly more evocative of AI & Law than making a toss-away reference to a robo-lawyer. Well, robo-judge comes pretty close too.

Note: *For supplemental materials depicting the aspects discussed in this chapter, refer to Appendix B, which contains various augmented diagrams, charts, and additional related facets of relevance.*

CHAPTER 4

AI & LAW:

LEGAL SINGULARITY

Key briefing points about this essay:

- A notable theory in AI is that someday there will be *The Singularity* (i.e., AI becomes sentient)

- No one can say for sure that this crossover into sentience will happen, nor when it might

- Some assert that the field of law will have its own AI moment known as the Legal Singularity

- It is useful to consider the ramifications of Legal Singularity to the law, the legal profession, etc.

- A leading and controversial hypothesis is that the law would no longer have any uncertainty

Introduction

Today's development of Artificial Intelligence (AI) is increasingly utilizing impressive techniques and technologies that attempt to mimic or simulate the nature of the human brain, incorporating the use of Artificial Neural Networks (ANNs) that are typically at the core of Machine Learning (ML) and Deep Learning (DL) efforts.

33

Despite some tremendous strides in crafting AI that appears to have a semblance of human intelligence, the reality currently is that contemporary AI is not remotely akin to the cognitive capabilities of the human mind.

In short, we are still abundantly far afield of achieving sentience in AI-based computer systems.

That being said, nonetheless, it is considered useful to contemplate what might happen if someday we do advance AI to the point of reaching sentience. The commonly accepted phrase that has emerged to denote this potential bridge crossing of AI becoming sentient is known as *The Singularity*.

Within the legal field, a variant of this same kind of threshold leap is known as the Legal Singularity. Legal scholars have discussed and debated the facets of what a Legal Singularity might consist of, along with postulating the logically plausible consequences that could arise.

In a moment, let's take a close look at what the Legal Singularity denotes and assess the hypothetical implications thereof.

First, it is instructive to dig more deeply into elements of the overarching *The Singularity* and see how that theory posits what will happen. We can then reassess those broader viewpoints and recast them into the specific context of the Legal Singularity.

Explaining The Singularity

How might the vaunted AI overarching instance of *The Singularity* occur?

Some assert that the way this will play out is that AI will fuel upon itself, generating a kind of intelligence explosion, and will spontaneously flourish toward becoming fully intelligent. Thus, rather than human beings toiling away at developing the AI into becoming this intelligent entity, a lower-threshold variant of AI will energize within itself and produce a heightened or pinnacle caliber of AI.

This is an interesting proposition since it opens the door to the possibility that we might not need to develop AI to this vaunted zenith on our own, and ergo only need to push the boundaries of AI up to whatever the threshold might be. One supposes that this makes life easier for AI developers, due to only having to progress AI to that initial trigger point. On the other hand, this also means that perhaps we are all in for a big shock, possibly due to having reached the threshold unexpectedly and astonishingly discover that we are then staring true AI in the face, as it were.

There are plenty of variants about *The Singularity*.

For example, it could be that the intelligence explosion goes much further than we imagined. Doing so might end-up producing not just everyday human quality intelligence, and instead might lead to super-intelligence. Nobody can say for sure what this super-intelligence might be able to do, other than apparently be smarter than any of us ordinary humans.

Another viewpoint is that the transition of the AI during this singularity will be a split second in time, less than the time that it takes to snap your fingers or blink your eyes, while others contend that the timeframe might be many seconds, or many minutes, or many days, or nearly any length of time to stew. Or, it could be that the AI reaches human intelligence quite quickly, but continues to percolate and over time gets smarter and smarter.

Explaining Legal Singularity

The discussion so far about *The Singularity* is considered with respect to general intelligence and overarching cognition and does not speak directly to anything per se about the law.

Suppose that AI has a similar type of singularity that applies specifically to the field of law, appropriately coined as the Legal Singularity.

What then?

Notice that this does not necessarily imply that *The Singularity* will have happened a priori, thus it is conceivable that the Legal Singularity might occur before there is the grandiose singularity. Some argue that it makes more sense to have the Legal Singularity arise after *The Singularity*. There are lots of back-and-forth arguments for either stance.

In any case, assume that the Legal Singularity does emerge.

One perspective is that this presumed Legal Singularity means there will be a semblance of AI that can do the same tasks as attorneys do, and the same work as judges, and otherwise perform any of the legal tasks that any human legal professional can do. As such, the question then surfaces that perhaps AI will in essence become the law profession, usurping any need for humans to perform the practice of law.

This outcome seems logically sensible if you buy into the notion that the AI will be at least equal to human intelligence. If humans can train to be lawyers and practice law, there would seem to be a reasonable claim that this AI could do likewise. Some assert that the AI would then be chosen by the public to undertake the tasks of the law, rather than having other humans do so. Perhaps the AI would be less costly to use, or more easily accessed, or in some means be a more compelling choice over the use of humans as a provisioner of legal services. One analogy is that if fully autonomous self-driving cars won't need human drivers, likewise fully autonomous AI-legal advisory systems will not need human attorneys (this assertion is debatable as an imperfect or ill-fitting analogy).

Not everyone perceives this future of the law as a mutually exclusive choice. They emphasize that the AI might work hand-in-hand (as it were) with human legal professionals. The public can choose to use the AI legal systems or use human lawyers, and in turn, the AI can choose to work with human lawyers as collaborators, while human lawyers can choose to utilize AI systems, all existing as legal equals.

On this provocative futuristic journey, there is another facet about the Legal Singularity that arises in these mechanizations. Some suggest that the law will inevitably become routinized by this AI advent. The AI will be so extensive that it will be able to encapsulate all manner and means of the law. Indeed, every possible permutation and combination of the law will be readily precalculated and determinable, and no surprises will remain.

Today's world of the law is said to be relatively uncertain, seemingly malleable, and ostensibly ill-defined, which will then dramatically shift via the AI into the law becoming solidified, perhaps one might say fossilized or petrified or ossified, removing any doubt or uncertainty about what the law portends. In that portrayal of the Legal Singularity, anytime a legal question arises, the matter is readily resolved by asking the AI what the answer is. Via a real-time on-demand and 24x7 accessible AI legal system, the hardest of legal questions can be nearly instantly answered, as can the more mundane legal matters.

One qualm expressed is that this implies the law would be unable to cope with the dynamics of the real-world to which the law is presumed to be applied, but the counter-argument is that you are falsely limiting the AI capacity in the sense that this "static" facet is not due to shortcutting what is possible, while instead, this remarkable AI has already anticipated all possibilities and therefore there aren't any new avenues or paths that have not already been considered. The totality of law will have been examined and exhaustively reasoned to all far corners and recesses that the law might extend.

Uncertain About Eradicating Uncertainty

How are you feeling about this prophesized Legal Singularity?

Some skeptics are extremely dubious that AI could inexorably wring out uncertainty from the law.

Consider a comparable scenario regarding the game of chess.

Chess consists of just a dozen or so unique player pieces and a rather petite set of rules. Today's AI that can compete at grandmaster levels does reasonably well, though there is not a guarantee of the AI winning and nor does the AI eliminate all uncertainty in the playing of the game. The number of variations of moves and countermoves is an exceedingly large search space, and the need for incorporating probabilities enters into the picture.

Even a futuristic AI that might ultimately best all human chess players is still unlikely to somehow unflaggingly eliminate uncertainty from chess playing. If this reduction of uncertainty to zero cannot be likely envisioned for chess, which is magnitudes more bounded than the vastness of the law, and the law inherently embodies semantic indeterminacy, why should AI be able to extract all uncertainty in legal matters?

The common rejoinder tends to invoke a hidden ace card in the deck, insisting that the AI upon reaching super-intelligence will be able to go far beyond what mere mortals can conceive. Presumably, this super-intelligence AI can find a path that will summarily dispatch uncertainty despite the objections raised by today's doubters.

Conclusion

What about the societal ramifications of the purported Legal Singularity?

Some assert that the specter of a Legal Singularity seems atrocious, gloomily foreshadowing a doomsday type of Dystopian scenario for society. Others opt to take the other side of that coin, claiming that a Utopian style outcome would emerge, so much so that we ought to be eagerly counting the days until the Legal Singularity duly materializes. Apt arguments on either side of this coin can be made, ranging from a joyous world vision of frictionless law or a downtrodden global handcuffing that makes the law into faceless automata ruing an iron fist over humanity.

Assuredly, the entire topic is at the outer boundaries of what we know today.

Unless a miraculous and early-bird AI spawning of the Legal Singularity suddenly appears, we seem to have plenty of time to do more deliberation about what to do and how we might shape the future. Presumably, the AI that we are crafting today is at the hands of mankind and *The Singularity* and the equally speculative Legal Singularity are still within our grasp to shape.

Note: *For supplemental materials depicting the aspects discussed in this chapter, refer to Appendix B, which contains various augmented diagrams, charts, and additional related facets of relevance.*

CHAPTER 5

AI & LAW:

LEGAL MICRO-DIRECTIVES

Key briefing points about this essay:

- Legal scholars have proposed that we might inevitably make use of legal micro-directives

- A legal micro-directive is a legal rule that goes beyond today's limited paper-based realm

- Envision a legal rule that is computer-based and able to be made available when needed

- In addition, ramp-up the computer-enablement by adding Artificial Intelligence (AI) into the mix

- This bodes for an era in which the law is smartly conveyed in real-time and decidedly on-point

Introduction

Legal scholars have been discussing with great intensity the possibility of a coming emergence of so-called legal micro-directives. As will be described herein, a legal micro-directive is essentially a legal rule that is enlivened by being computer-based and inevitably AI-powered (note: not everyone necessarily agrees on this particular definition, so please be aware that other variants exist).

Currently, a legal rule is usually paper-based, hidden from view, hard to find, unavailable when needed, and otherwise trapped in an information glutted morass.

In the future, legal rules will be readily present, instantly accessible, and proactively brought to everyday matters by automation that proffers the right legal rule at the right time and place. This newer and more invigorated form of a legal rule is generally referred to as a legal micro-directive.

Notice that this does not necessarily mean that the legal micro-directives are created by the automation.

It is easy to get the two aspects mixed into the same stew. Humans could still devise the legal micro-directives and the automation merely serves them up when relevant to do so. Thus, humanity is still making laws. The automation is aiding in conveying the laws and boosting awareness and presumably complying with the laws.

Sometimes there is an inadvertent convoluting of the messenger with the originator, in the sense that if the computer is delivering the legal micro-directive this ergo seemingly implies that the automation devised the legal micro-directive. This does not have to be the case. Lawmakers can figure out the laws that are needed, and then the automation can aid in transforming those laws into the appropriate set of legal micro-directives, along with storing the legal micro-directives and sharing them throughout society.

Popular Examples Of Legal Micro-Directives

One of the most frequently cited examples of leveraging legal micro-directives involves the lawful act of driving a car.

Today, you glance at a posted speed limit sign to figure out what is the allowed speed on a given roadway (if you can spot it, and if it hasn't been damaged or marred).

Imagine instead that your car has an electronic display console and there is a roadway computer-based system emitting a message to the in-car display that says the local speed limit in that area is 35 miles per hour (some jurisdictions are already putting this V2I, vehicle-to-infrastructure, capability in place).

That's an example of a legal rule, in this case, considered a legal micro-directive, delivered to the point of need at the right time and right place. A person driving a car doesn't have to try and randomly guess what the speed limit is, nor resort to looking it up in a directory. A roadway piece of electronic infrastructure, embodying appropriate legal micro-directives in a repository, serves forth a message to passing cars as they proceed along on the road. Furthermore, if there are other lawful instructions regarding that street or byway about perhaps barring left turns or other facets, those too would be sent to the vehicle.

Consider another example.

You are in the midst of building an addition to your cherished home. It is all too easy to undertake a modest modification of a patched roof or deck and find out later on that some arcane and insidious legal rules were covering those changes. Imagine that while on-site at your domicile and examining the proposed alterations, your smartphone might receive a series of automatically generated messages from the local home construction regulations department, indicating pertinent legal micro-directives that need to be abided. Those messages arrive in real-time at the point of need, rather than having to go down to the city hall offices to try and unearth the legal rules or otherwise ferret them out.

Significance Of Legal Micro-Directives

You might be tempted to think that the advent of legal micro-directives doesn't seem that special and appears to be rather humdrum.

Isn't this merely the transmission of legal rules?

Well, that would be a narrow way to view the capabilities envisioned. Legal scholars would heartily suggest that such a first glance is woefully undercutting the tremendous impact that legal micro-directives will have on legal institutional power, encompassing moral and ethical consequences for day-to-day citizens, particularly in their relationship to lawmakers and the government.

There will be a reduced amount of friction, as it were, between lawmaking and the emission of the ascertained laws. This frictionless path would allow for new laws to nearly instantaneously be put into use. No long delays and no bulky lawbooks or hefty tranches of legislation that by design or by happenstance contain buried legal rules that are akin to ticking timebombs to someday be encountered.

Undeniably, there is a two-sided sword to this matter.

The pace of providing laws and getting them into active use will be amazingly timely and fast-acting. On the other hand, will citizens that are bound by these legal micro-directives be overwhelmed by a deluge of constantly changing and perpetually appearing legal rules? Their reaction is sure to be equally swift, reacting to the micro-directives by responding immediately to the lawmakers that generated them.

Some also assert that the generated AI-powered legal micro-directives will be more complete and far-reaching than conventional legal rules tend to be.

The good news might be that you can right away discover the entire range of legal conditions and lawful limitations associated with that new addition to your home that is being constructed. This could include legal rules that nobody would have normally figured out, yet the automation, when boosted with AI, was able to do so. In short, the AI is presumably going to take the essence of any overarching legal goals and turn them into a comprehensive set of legal micro-directives, covering a wide array of possibilities that lawmakers did not necessarily consider on their own.

That's handy to detect and avert any legal loopholes that otherwise would be inadvertently formed via the error-prone manual writing of laws.

Of course, the potentially disturbing news is that the AI could mechanistically derive legal micro-directives that were not bound within the intentions of the lawmakers. If a legal goal was broadly defined by lawmakers, and the AI-spawned multitudes of legal micro-directives that are voluminous and painstakingly specific, something could go astray. In that manner, the AI could be accused of creating new law, going beyond the scope of merely delivering it.

For some, that is a bridge too far.

How To Create Legal Micro-Directives

One means to handle such adverse consequences involves having the AI-generated legal micro-directives cycle back to the lawmakers for their final review and approval.

The AI would start by initially receiving a broadly based legal goal, generate the set of legal micro-directives, and then funnel those back to the lawmakers to make sure nothing got lost in the translation. In some respects, this could jog the lawmakers into realizing they had neglected to consider aspects of the proposed laws that would have inevitably been found at a later date. And, at that later date, this would have likely consumed the judicial processes as to what the law was meant to indicate.

A potential implication is that the amount of legal wrangling and the use of the judicial approach to adjudicating the law would drop precipitously due to the upfront nature of legal micro-directives. Whether this would do away with judges and lawyering is not something being devoutly discussed, but it is floated as a presumed potential decrease in the amount of litigation and, therefore, a reduced overall need for litigators.

A dizzying dystopian view of the legal micro-directive concept is that the AI decides to do a takeover. Maybe the AI becomes smart enough or sentient and decides that rather than being the "middle man" between the lawmakers and the citizens, it can become the lawmaker. The citizens are already used to getting the legal micro-directives from the AI, so cutting out the lawmakers from this tight loop might seem easy and sneakily invisible to the citizenry.

To pile onto the dystopian view, another concern is the preordained or precognition use of legal micro-directives as alluded to in the movie *Minority Report* starring Tom Cruise. Suppose a surgeon is going to perform a surgery, and the potential negligence is rated as high, such that a legal micro-directive is sent to the medical-surgical devices and automatically set to disallow the medical operation. How far will the use of legal micro-directives go?

Generally, those outstretched concerns entailing a proverbial off-the-rails possibility are downplayed by those advocating the legal micro-directives benefits, suggesting that those doomsday portrayals are in a fantastical and improbable realm. They would assert that you could just as readily make utopian scenarios that are similarly extreme, suggesting that the legal micro-directives will cure all of society's ills. It seems that in whatever manner you might view AI-enabled legal micro-directives, there can be a conjured case made for their being valued, and meanwhile a countering case for them to be reviled.

Conclusion

For the time being, AI-embellished legal micro-directives are an innovation that we prudently ought to walk-before-we-run as to employing such a dramatically outsized new legal accouterment. Pragmatism dictates that we might wish to ease our way into the introduction of AI-based legal micro-directives while simultaneously keeping a circumspect eye on untoward outcomes.

That poignant advice seems like a lawfully mindful micro-directive worthwhile to be embraced.

———————

Note: *For supplemental materials depicting the aspects discussed in this chapter, refer to Appendix B, which contains various augmented diagrams, charts, and additional related facets of relevance.*

CHAPTER 6
AI & LAW:
LEGAL ARGUMENTATION

Key briefing points about this essay:

- One might boldly suggest that humans are essentially biologically-based arguing machines

- Besides our general propensity to argue, argumentation in the law is a paramount skill

- Artificial Intelligence (AI) is going to increasingly be utilized for legal argumentation purposes

- There are four primary ways that AI-enabled legal reasoning will be used in argumentation

- The gradual expansion of AI in the law will serve to powerfully enhance legal argumentation

Introduction

There seems to be something innate in humanity that we are able to argue. Indeed, it would seem that we oftentimes delight in arguing. As with most salient aspects of our various cognitive acts, there are problematic considerations when trying to distinctly ascertain whether our compulsion to argue is due to DNA, or whether it is a skill that we acquire during our lifetimes.

Overall, arguing might be imputed via nature or nurture, or perhaps an inseparable combination of the two.

There are many contexts in which arguing and the role of argumentation arise. In the case of the law, there are voluminous treatises about the form and formulation of legal argumentation. Scholars have attempted to dissect the very fabric upon which legal argumentation rests. Law schools stridently seek to guide budding attorneys toward the bright light of refined and highly seasoned legal argumentation.

Let it be said, if not overly obvious, that legal argumentation is crucial to our adversarial form of justice.

Cooked into the very stew of justice and ingrained indelibly throughout the judicial process, we use legal argumentation as a means to seek intrinsically optimal or sufficiently best-possible outcomes. Presumably, the more robust that competing legal arguments can go head-to-head, the greater the chances of arriving at a just conclusion. If one side proffers a weaker legal argument, the assumption is that it will fail to convince, and thus the stronger legal argument will prevail.

Where can computers and especially the advent of Artificial Intelligence (AI) come to play in this daily and ongoing battle utilizing legal argumentation?

This is an important question and bodes for the future of the law, given that the practice of law will inevitably imbue the application of AI-powered legal reasoning systems.

Legal Argumentation And The CARE Model

In my research on AI and legal argumentation, I've identified four keyways that legal argumentation is being augmented via advanced automation.

These four essentials are coined via the convenient acronym of CARE, entailing Crafting, Assessing, Refining, and Engaging. These distinct actions represent the overall means by which LegalTech experts and legal scholars are making use of or attempting to infuse AI Legal Argumentation (AILA) capabilities into the practice of law and the furtherance of the legal profession.

Let's briefly consider each of the four key actions.

The first of the noted actions or activities involves *crafting* a legal argument.

When a seasoned lawyer initially takes on a case, they tend to instinctively begin mulling over the legal position that they anticipate undertaking, thusly sifting through the elements of legal arguments that will underlie the case. This eventually blossoms and maturates into a larger overarching collection of legal arguments which are then coalesced into a cohesive whole.

For newbie lawyers, there is oftentimes a substantive chance that the legal arguments being brought together are unable to readily be fashioned into a unified whole (you might recall in law school struggling with composing your IRAC, describing the Issue, Rule, Application, Conclusion). At times, the novice lawyer cannot ferret out the forest for the trees. Also, they might have anchored themselves onto legal arguments that are potentially irrelevant to the case or that otherwise distract from the true core of the matter at hand. That's not to suggest that even experienced lawyers cannot fall into the same mental traps, namely that they can, and do so, but there is usually a stronger probability that they will catch themselves before the fashioning gets too far along.

If possible, efforts to construct a robust legal argument are oftentimes bolstered by seeking the opinions and review of trusted colleagues. Presumably, by sharing a coalescing legal argument with fellow lawyers and partners, it is expected that any gaps, loopholes, or innate argumentation failings will be detected and resolved.

The overarching goal is to produce a maximally vigorous legal argument, particularly since the opposing side will undoubtedly be aiming to find any otherwise undiscovered gotchas. Better to identify your own argumentation weaknesses beforehand, rather than having your head handed to you by the opposing side.

This is where the use of AI especially comes to the fore.

Various AI-enabled legal argumentation tools are being built and deployed to aid in serving as an over-the-shoulder aid when *assessing* the strength of a proposed legal argument.

Such AI attempts to ascertain whether there are omissions or inconsistencies in the legal argument logic. By flagging those potential problems, the human lawyer can be sparked into realizing any logic traps that they have inadvertently fallen into and seek to rectify those before proffering their legal argumentation to others.

Even more advanced is the capability of the AI for *refining* legal arguments.

Rather than simply identifying or assessing where legal arguments might be deficient, the refinement capability provides hints or suggestions of what ought to be improved. In fact, if extensively advanced, the AI offers outright indications of the best possible refinements to be made.

Lastly, in terms of the CARE aspects, there is the *engaging* facet, consisting of an interactive dialogue of the AI in conjunction with the human lawyer, allowing for real-time Natural Language Processing (NLP) dialogue and debate about the legal argumentation. In a sense, this can act as a practice session, allowing the lawyer to tryout the legal arguments and see what responses the opposing side might attempt, though doing so in a simulated environment and without the risks associated with toe-to-toe opponent skirmishes.

Today's Reality Of AI-Powered Legal Argumentation

Before you whisk out your credit card to purchase any such AI-enabled legal argumentation toolset, be aware that most of these efforts are still quite exploratory and tend to be exceedingly research-oriented. Let it be known that creating a good legal argument is indubitably hard work and getting AI to do so is devilishly difficult. Assessing a legal argument is also onerous, being quite problematic for today's AI capabilities.

The same can be said for AI that attempts to refine legal arguments. Perhaps especially difficult is carrying on a fluid and seemingly informed dialogue or debate, the engaging activity, as it entails direct AI-to-human interaction and, as might be evident from today's Siri and Alexa, there is still a long way to go before NLP is truly proficient and fluent.

The application of AI to legal argumentation will gradually be improved (there seems little doubt about that trend). Indeed, some are worried that eventually, AI will take over legal argumentation entirely, as though we might end-up with AI arguing against AI in our courtrooms, rather than human lawyers arguing with fellow human lawyers. This is a rather futuristic prophecy, and you can stop losing sleep at night worrying about it, for now.

On a realistic bent, there is a much greater chance that we'll sooner see the use of AI Legal Argumentation as a handy tool for lawyers, boosting their legal argumentation skills and readying them for trial and the deployment of their legal arguments. Thus, in the foreseeable future, AI for legal argumentation will be relatively mechanistic and serve as a spading tool for lawyers. This involves aspects such as storing catalogs and snippets of legal arguments, enabling their online access. To some degree, this also will encompass indications of which legal arguments tend to fit with others, and which are considered counterpoints.

Via the use of AI capabilities encompassing Machine Learning and Deep Learning, drafted legal arguments will be classified into categorizations indicating their potency and relevancy, along with aiding in predicting which logic-based attacks might be successfully employed against those arguments. Likewise, this will assist in finding serialized attack points, referred to as attack vectors, regarding the legal arguments of the opposing side.

Conclusion

Shifting gears, there's an intriguing additional perspective regarding why it makes abundant sense to blend AI and argumentation.

If arguing is indeed a fundamental tenet of humans, you could assert that argumentation is crucial to human intelligence.

Keep in mind that the goal of those in the AI field consists of trying to make computers that can exhibit human intelligence, and therefore one can logically deduce that infusing argumentation capabilities into AI might demonstrably aid in pushing the technology closer and closer toward displaying human-like intelligent capacities. Interestingly, getting AI to be argumentative could be the missing link toward achieving AI's ultimate aspirations. Furthermore, legal argumentation, in particular, turns out to be one of the richest sources of argumentation and ergo a focus of AI not solely due to the interest in law, but because legal argumentation raises the art form and to some degree the science of arguing.

Perhaps that might make you feel better the next time you make a misstep in a legal argument for a case, knowing that nonetheless you are perceived as a stellar argument-making and argument-professing human, for which AI is "envious" and aiming to catch up with you.

May all your legal arguments be fruitful and unassailable.

Note: *For supplemental materials depicting the aspects discussed in this chapter, refer to Appendix B, which contains various augmented diagrams, charts, and additional related facets of relevance.*

CHAPTER 7

AI & LAW:

PRINCIPLES OF JUSTICE

Key briefing points about this essay:

- Artificial Intelligence (AI) will undoubtedly continue to be integrated into the practice of law

- Some suggest this will undercut a semblance of justice, while others say it will bolster justice

- A sensible place to start such a discussion involves defining *justice* (using key precepts)

- AI legal reasoning systems can apply to each of the defined seven principles of justice

- Ascertaining the ultimate outcome of applying AI will be up to how we choose to proceed

Introduction

Artificial Intelligence (AI) is increasingly being immersed in the field of law. Some speak of the advent of so-called robo-lawyers and robo-judges. Depending upon the perspective of a particular pundit, the application of AI for legal reasoning is either going to be a boon for justice or will be the demise of justice.

In short, a vital question being asked is whether the ongoing and futuristic AI-enabled legal reasoning systems will inexorably produce a Utopian-style form of justice or lead to a disastrous Dystopian era of appalling legal misery for us all?

Let's consider first what it means to refer to justice and then mindfully examine how online lawyering and how AI-enabled LegalTech can be a powerful one-two punch to bolster access-to-justice and reshape a myriad of legal mechanizations aiming to strengthen the future of legal wellbeing.

The Core Principles of Justice

An excellent book by Professor Richard Susskind entitled "Online Courts and the Future of Justice" lays out the carefully established case that justice can be generally cast as consisting of seven core principles. Based on those key principles, he convincingly argues that online courts will both preserve justice and enhance justice, doing so via the prudent utilization of virtual hearings, plus asynchronous online judging, and so on. He rightfully forewarns that it is not a foregone conclusion that these benefits will arise and that it will require sensible, determined, and systemic multi-generational adaptations to get there.

In a nutshell, here is a quick paraphrasing of the seven identified principles underlying justice:

- **Substantive Justice:** Decisions and outcomes should be considered fair and substantive, requiring judging to be based on the laws of the land and not by whim or other divines.

- **Procedural Justice:** The process needs to be equitable and honest, independent of biases, and proffer procedures that avert the incursion of defectiveness or inconsistencies.

- **Open Justice:** Efforts of the courts must be transparent, open to scrutiny, accountable, and intelligible, avoiding secrecy as much as can be so reasonably achieved (realizing that at times national security, the welfare of minors, and the like can motivate some degrees of confidentiality).

- **Distributive Justice:** Each person must be given their legal due and afforded access to justice, thus driving a semblance of distributiveness to ensure that regardless of means that all can gain access.

- **Proportionate Justice:** Fairness ought to arise at scale, straightforward processes for straightforward issues, attempting to ensure that speediness occurs and aligns too with complexity, suitable proportionality based on the assertion that justice delayed is justice diluted.

- **Enforceable Justice:** Results need to have teeth and be seen as binding, enforcement as enabled via the coercive power of the state, correctly deprive money and property and liberty to ensure justice is served.

- **Sustainable Justice:** Have a stable basis for the ongoing instantiation of justice, sufficient resources must be allocated to maintain and incur upkeep for continually improving the means of the courts to act, including being able to demonstrably scale to whatever volume of cases might be presented.

Note that the seven principles are not numbered and nor otherwise indicated as being prioritized or ranked in any particular order. They are all equally crucial. Imagine a three-legged stool that falls apart when any of the legs is missing, though in this instance envisage a seven-legged apparatus. There are tradeoffs among the principles, and it is not easy to ensure that they are each given their full and earnestly needed equal attention.

Keep in mind that existing attempts at justice are not necessarily able to live up to the ideals of the stated principles, and thus today's form of justice is undeniably at times existent of numerous shortcomings, including being too costly, taking too long, being unintelligible for many that rely upon the law, etc.

This emphasizes that today's barometer of justice is not somehow already presaged at the topmost stance. If it were, the addition or incorporation of innovation such as online capabilities could be argued as potentially messing with perfection, but this is not the case per se. Online infusion offers a chance of improving the day-to-day incurring and delivery of justice. In that same vein, if online options are badly integrated, the existing justice system could be degraded, dropping from the remarkable perch it currently resides at. Susskind offers an extensive explanation showcasing how online courts and online lawyering can enliven the core principles of justice.

Intertwining AI And The Justice Principles

Shifting gears, consider how AI can impact justice, and either embolden the core principles or if inappropriately applied could damage justice.

For example, AI-enabled Machine Learning could be utilized to aid in bolstering the *Substantive Justice* principle as a means to assess whether legal decisions are fair with respect to the law, comparing the text and meaning of laws themselves to the human judging decisions made, and comparing the human judging decisions in contrast to like decisions by fellow human judges.

When making this suggestion, some will instantly recoil at the thought that AI is stepping into the role of making judicial judgments, which to be abundantly clear is not the case being made here.

Though there are assuredly speculations that we might eventually find ourselves making use of so-called robo-judges, that's a far distance from today's AI and it is not even well-established that AI, if so equipped, would be desirably placed into such bearings (a rousing topic that continues to be embroiled in AI Ethics quarters).

The case being made here is that the AI could be a tool to aid in conducting these kinds of legal analyses, ultimately being run and interpreted by humans to help gauge how well *Substantive Justice* is being observed. The laborious nature of such an undertaking could be reduced via the wise application of AI, and offer a more efficacious means to cope with the existing volume of legal efforts and handle the predicted heightened volume that our courts are likely to experience.

That being said, if the AI is poorly devised and creates too many false positives (alerting unfairness when the matter is better construed as being fair), or an excessive amount of false negatives (letting unfairness skate through undetected), the AI could worsen the situation, due to an anthropomorphic assumption that the AI "must be right" and therefore is unduly relied upon.

Tackling briefly another example, consider the impact of AI on *Distributive Justice.*

Suppose that via online facilities, access to justice is boosted and becomes more abundantly distributed. The question arises as to whether the everyday layperson will even realize that their online access can empower them to undertake suitable legal actions or seek lawful remedies.

In other words, they might stare hopelessly at a blank screen, without any inkling of what their legal rights are and incapable to pursue them, thus the vaunted access is regrettably shallow and symbolic rather than functional and practical.

One aspect that could sharpen the access usage would be the deployment of AI-powered legal chatbots.

The layperson at their otherwise blank screen might be prompted with questions from the AI component, asking in an easily understood Natural Language Processing (NLP) dialogue what kind of legal problem the person perhaps is confronting. Initial information could be collected and the AI chatbot via its capabilities would diagnose whether the matter is within the realm of likely legal pursuits.

A qualm fervently expressed by some is that this is tantamount to practicing law and the AI is usurping the role of properly credentialed and authorized attorneys. There is an ongoing debate in the courts and the legal profession as to what constitutes the practice of law, and as such, it is not necessarily the case that the mere act of collecting info and doing some initial diagnoses is, in fact, the practice of law, but in any case, note that the AI chatbot would presumably be reporting its info to a human attorney. Thus, it could be argued that the AI chatbot is a mechanism or tool for lawyers, rather than a replacement or substitute for an attorney (admittedly, this is a quagmire that still needs to be settled).

This last point also brings up the confusion that some have about AI as though it is an all-knowing all-seeing autonomous capability. Per my research, it is prudent to consider AI as varying along a spectrum from rather limited simple automation and progressing to someday becoming fully advanced autonomy, thus having varying impacts depending upon the degree of what is referred to as Levels of Autonomy (LoA) for the use of AI in legal reasoning.

Conclusion

All told, the core principles of justice provide a vital sketch of what needs to be at the forefront of any tech-fueled innovations in the legal field. It is commonplace to get caught up in the fever of new tech, especially AI LegalTech, and do so without somber regard to how justice will be served or potentially undermined by employing such advances.

Try to keep the lucky number seven in mind and have handy the key principles whenever getting excessively starry-eyed at the latest legal gadgetry.

———

Note: *For supplemental materials depicting the aspects discussed in this chapter, refer to Appendix B, which contains various augmented diagrams, charts, and additional related facets of relevance.*

CHAPTER 8

AI & LAW:

REENGINEERING THE LAW

Key briefing points about this essay:

- An oft saying in the tech field is that you should stridently avoid paving the cow paths

- This catchy phrase asserts that you must do reengineering before adopting new technologies

- This matters because many of today's legal ways in the courts and in law firms are outmoded

- Meanwhile, new tech such as AI is merely being plunked on top of those "as is" processes

- Hoped-for gains and value from AI-based LegalTech must be accompanied by reengineering

Introduction

There is an old saying among those in the tech field that you should never pave the cow paths.

Here's what that means.

First, let's define cow paths. For those of you that have ever driven the streets of Boston, you'll likely know how wildly winding and twisty those Bostonian roads are. One-way boulevards appear to inexplicably do loop de loops, while many paths seem to be designed by a demented roadway engineer that sought to make the driving as arduous and confounding as possible (successfully so). Well, it wasn't a mad scientist that did the trickery, instead, it was the cows.

In the early days of the formation of Boston, early settlers would bring their cows to town and also walk them back out to the countryside. Turns out that cows go wherever they want to go, meaning that they would meander while being generally guided, and thus Boston had lots of intersecting and ultimately well-worn dirt paths.

When it came time to plunk down asphalt to make way for vehicular traffic, the approach consisted of paving those very same cow paths.

Some cities are based on a shrewdly devised grid approach, consisting of streets and avenues, arranged perpendicular to each other. This allows for a rather straightforward form of navigation, along with making it easy to stipulate where a house or a building is located, using a simple coordinate convention.

Not so when the roads are weaving to and fro.

The lesson to be gleaned is that when you are going to make a change, especially a large-scale one, such as laying down the pavement and thus "freezing in" whatever is there, take a close look at how things have been done to date, and reflect carefully upon whether you first might want to reengineer or redesign the way things are and reimagine how they ought to be.

The Cow Paths Of Our Legal Ways

We can now shift our attention to a particular application of tech, namely the use of tech in the law, typically referred to as LegalTech or LawTech. When implementing modern-day technology for law practices and the courts, we need to consider employing the same handy rule-of-thumb: *Do not pave the cow paths.* Unfortunately, this insightful mantra is rarely observed.

There is a decidedly and frequent lack of awareness about the "as is" versus the "to be" within law firms and inside our courts when reaching out to buy and jam into place the latest new technology. Rather than closely examining their existing processes and figuring out how to become more effective and efficient by leveraging the tech, i.e., simultaneously redoing those well-worn activities, the lazy or ill-informed approach involves simply trying to automate the way things have always been done.

Case closed.

Unfortunately, the odds are unnervingly high that this will undermine the benefits expected from the likely costly investment in the adopted technology and leave the office partners or the court authorities baffled about why after the gargantuan sized investments there are few if any garnered improvements and the entities still seem inexplicably unable to be snappier about conducting their legal efforts.

The sober anecdote about the cow paths is timely because we are about to enter into a post-COVID era that opens the question about how technology can be best adapted to enact a new normal for our legal system.

Reengineering Being Called For

The shock of the coronavirus impact has brought forth a time of reckonings, as emphatically pointed out by my colleague Professor David Freeman at the Stanford Law School and his co-author Bridget Mary McCormack, Chief Justice of the Michigan Supreme Court, in a piece recently entitled "Courts will need to adapt to the coronavirus crush" as posted at Bloomberg Opinion on July 15, 2020.

The reckonings they refer to are all around us each day, including that the existing legal system was and still is ill-prepared for a now prescribed online and remote-work ecosystem, one that would allow the involved parties to participate in the pursuit of justice without having to physically endure coming to a courtroom and be endangered by the life-threatening possibilities of an infectious outcome to their case.

There is also a perilously dangling reckoning associated with the anticipated tsunami of cases that will soon flood our courts amid numerous pandemic-related fallouts such as the lifting of the moratorium on evictions. There is going to be a cacophony of spurred cases arising from the multi-headed serpent of COVID-19 that will play out in our economy, in business, and in our lives, much of which will land into the courts.

And we all know that the courts already were busting at the seams.

When reflecting on the coming turbulent seas, the co-authors deftly proffered an astute call-to-order: "How we face this reckoning — with business as usual, or with new thinking about who can provide legal services and new technologies that assist in that work — will help chart the future of our justice system and determine whether it serves us all or just a few."

For those willing and daring enough to embrace such an exhortation toward new thinking, I would like to add that we must do so without paving those outmoded cow paths.

Prudent application of LegalTech, when combined with AI capabilities, can dramatically widen access to our courts and provide a viable means to deal with the coming deluge of legal requests and co-commitment consumption of needed legal services.

Lawyers must be electronically armed appropriately and so too must legal assistants, leveraging all of their day-to-day legal efforts via online platforms, along with utilizing the latest in AI-enabled discovery tools, legal chatbots, and the like.

Judges and the courts must equally enter into this AI-empowered realm, willingly adopting such technologies that are already available and giving due attention to those emerging ones that are coming down the pike.

Among the likely expected angst and haste to do so, we must all first make sure to consider how existing practices are paper-based and manually ingrained, which does not necessarily lend itself to being automated as is. There needs to be mindful introspection and review, along with reengineering, none of which is going to be heralded at the time, and principally will be painful, but in the end, the result will be worth it.

Conclusion

The time is ripe to restructure and reimagine the cow paths of our legal system, aiming to shift into gear for a modern age and transform toward a future that is ultimately going to intrinsically interleave AI and ubiquitous technology into all facets of our lives.

Note: *For supplemental materials depicting the aspects discussed in this chapter, refer to Appendix B, which contains various augmented diagrams, charts, and additional related facets of relevance.*

CHAPTER 9

AI & LAW:

LEGAL SENTIMENTALITY

Key briefing points about this essay:

- Questions abound about the role of sentimentality and emotion with the halls of justice

- A famous court case entailing a *Tribute to a Dog* is legendary for a sentimental closing argument

- AI can be utilized to try and gauge sentimentality within a written record of a court case

- There is also the use of AI for real-time sentimentality detection and for opinion mining

- The future could entail using AI routinely in this rooting out the role, but qualms remain

Introduction

Let's consider how sentimentality can be intertwined into the courts, though presumably there is supposedly no place for sappiness or emotional turpitude therein.

One of the most revered closing arguments in an American courtroom took place in 1870 as part of the now-classic court case *Burden v Hornsby*. The eloquent remarks became known as the famed *Tribute to a Dog*. This is the heartwarming moniker given to the closing argument proffered by the lawyer representing Charles Burden, powerfully elucidated by Missouri attorney and statesman George Graham Vest, and for which has been noted in history as one of the most celebrated or perhaps infamous closing statements ever made in an American courtroom.

Here is the text of the opening paragraph for Vest's somewhat soppy closing argument:

> "The best friend a man has in the world may turn against him and become his enemy. His son or daughter that he has reared with loving care may prove ungrateful. Those who are nearest and dearest to us, those whom we trust with our happiness and our good name may become traitors to their faith. The money that a man has, he may lose. It flies away from him, perhaps when he needs it most. A man's reputation may be sacrificed in a moment of ill-considered action. The people who are prone to fall on their knees to do us honor when success is with us may be the first to throw the stone of malice when failure settles its cloud upon our heads."

No dogs are mentioned in there as yet, but we are being set up by the contention that people are not necessarily loyal to one another, and that indeed people seem pretty much to be entirely out for themselves and utterly unreliable and undependable.

Given that setting of the stage, as it were, here's the next part of Vest's commentary:

> "The one absolutely unselfish friend that man can have in this selfish world, the one that never deserts him, the one that never proves ungrateful or treacherous is his dog. A man's dog stands by him in prosperity and in poverty, in health and in sickness. He will sleep on the cold ground,

where the wintry winds blow and the snow drives fiercely, if only he may be near his master's side. He will kiss the hand that has no food to offer. He will lick the wounds and sores that come in encounters with the roughness of the world. He guards the sleep of his pauper master as if he were a prince. When all other friends desert, he remains. When riches take wings, and reputation falls to pieces, he is as constant in his love as the sun in its journey through the heavens."

And so on, the closing argument prattles along in that same vein.

Upon reading even just the first two paragraphs of his remarks, I wouldn't blame you if you rushed home right away to hug your beloved pet dog or maybe drove directly over to your local pet store to obtain a venerated canine. I realize that cat lovers might be a bit chagrined at all this love being tossed toward dogs and feel left out, but do keep in mind that the court case dealt with a hunting dog named "Old Drum" that Burden owned and that was shot dead by a sheep farmer named Leonidas Hornsby. Vest was trying to urge the jury toward awarding Buren a requested $150 judgment (the jury allotted $50; the case was appealed by Hornsby and eventually landed at the Missouri Supreme Court, with Burden prevailing).

Besides being a popular and long-lasting tribute to dogs, there is something else notable about this particular closing argument: *There was nothing whatsoever mentioned in the closing statement about the case per se.*

Vest did not discuss the evidence. He did not bring up the various facets of the case and nor deal with any contentions or counterarguments underlying the matters at hand. Instead, he delivered an impassioned speech that was vacuous of any demonstrative legal substance. Admittedly, he won the case, and thus presumably the closing argument was sufficient, though it is of course hard to say how much those sentimental statements impacted the decision made by the jurors. Could things have turned out better if Vest had made sure to include legal substances? Maybe, maybe not. Unless there is a parallel universe in which we can do a redo, we'll never know for sure.

Doggedness Of Sentimentality

Shift gears and consider the nature of your legal efforts.

In theory, the law and the practice of law are supposed to take place in an atmosphere of objectivity, devoid of any passion, feelings, or similar sentiments. The facts are the facts, and any subjectivity is to be inextricably and inexorably weeded out of the matter. Logic shall prevail over whim or gut instinct.

But is that what really happens?

There is undoubtedly and seeming inarguably an infusion of sentiment into nearly every nook and cranny of how the practice of law takes place. Some would vehemently point out that humans are humans, meaning that since the practice of law and the efforts of the courts is undertaken by humans, you have to assume and expect that human emotions and sentiment will be awash throughout the process. There is no getting around it.

That being the case, if you accept that claimed premise, the obvious next step is to try and ferret out the inclusion of sentiment and bring it to the fore. If there is going to a systematic notion of mitigating or eliminating sentiment from the proceedings, you have to first detect that it exists and is being utilized. After making a detection, you can then decide what course of action to take in dealing with mitigating or eradicating it.

Enter into this picture the use of sentiment analysis, oftentimes formally referred to as Sentiment Analysis (SA) and considered a field of study that embodies techniques from linguistics, social behavioral science, psychology, and the like. In brief, sentiment analysis seeks to examine any kind of expression and ascertain whether there is sentiment included and what kind of sentiment is being used.

This can include interpreting facial expressions, such as trying to ascertain whether a person is happy or sad, angry or contented, and so on, doing so via the look on their face.

This can also be done by the words a person uses while speaking. Sentiment can arise in the words chosen and the intonation made while uttering those words. In addition, sentiment can be found within the written word, allowing for perusing a written narrative to seek out the sentiment embedded within any given prose.

Turns out that the by-hand approaches to Sentiment Analysis are increasingly being bolstered by Artificial Intelligence (AI).

Modern-day AI can examine images of collected facial expressions to try and determine which sentiments underly those visual indications. AI can examine voice recordings and do analyses even during a live stream of someone speaking, doing so to flush out the sentiment. Today's AI can also inspect written texts and try to spot sentiment that might be hidden within the narrative provided.

There is an allied area known as Opinion Mining (OM). Some assert that SA and OM are synonymous and therefore treat them as the same thing. Others contend that SA is about feelings or emotions, while an opinion is more akin to a narrative that is either factually based or non-factually based, and thus OM is distinct from SA. Whether they are separable or not, most would nonetheless concede that they are close cousins of each other and oftentimes work hand-in-hand.

Another variant is whether the sentiment or opinions are being uncovered in just any kind of expression or whether it is an expression found within a legal context. Recall the *Tribute to a Dog* and consider the remarks that were made by attorney Vest, doing so in a legal context during the closing arguments of the case. You might say that he used a form of legal sentiment and a form of legal "opinion" in how he elucidated his closing remarks.

Immersed Into AI And The Law

In my research on AI and the law, I define SA and OM in a legal context and consider them as separate but aligned topics:

- *Legal Sentiment Analysis (LSA) entails the detection of expressed or implied sentiment about a legal matter within the context of a legal milieu.*

- *Legal Opinion Mining (LOM) entails the identification and illumination of explicit or implicit opinion accompaniments immersed within legal discourse.*

Gradually, advances in AI will allow the law profession to make use of Legal Sentiment Analysis and Legal Opinion Mining to increasingly expanded uses. To what end, you might wonder? The notion is that LSA and LOM can be used in a variety of significant and notable ways. A written court case and its judgment could be reviewed by an AI system capable of performing sufficient LSA and LOM to try and assess where sentiment and opinion reside (differentiating "opinion" of a factual nature versus that of a non-factually based nature). This might be used to be better informed about the nature of the case and might even be used as a basis for appeal.

Here's the scarier part, perhaps, which will potentially become apparent in the next few years.

As the courts go online, partially sparked by trying to contend with the pandemic, it will be relatively easy to leverage an AI-based sentiment analyzer during a trial. The online video could be examined in real-time by the AI system, examining the expressions of the judge, the jury, the attorneys, expert witnesses, and the like. An attorney using such technology could be getting real-time updates from the AI about the sentiments being expressed, leveraging those insights accordingly.

Some are worried that this opens a Pandora's box and believe it is yet another reason to go slowly in terms of having the courts become online based. Others contend that this kind of AI-powered technology is inevitably going to weave its way into the practice of law and that trying to keep it at bay is a head-in-the-sand perspective.

Conclusion

Aristotle philosophized that the law should be free of passion. Imagine his reaction at seeing today's world and our judicial approaches, and one wonders whether he would be in favor of adopting AI-enabled Legal Sentiment Analysis and Legal Opinion Mining, or whether he would make an impassioned argument against it.

Either way, this kind of AI is coming along and will undeniably become a force to be reckoned with. Meanwhile, remain calm and see if you can find a puppy someplace to pet and play with, it might help to reduce the unnerving reaction to these rather disquieting matters.

Note: *For supplemental materials depicting the aspects discussed in this chapter, refer to Appendix B, which contains various augmented diagrams, charts, and additional related facets of relevance.*

CHAPTER 10

AI & LAW:

THREE TIERS OF LAW

Key briefing points about this essay:

- Currently, the practice of law is tightly controlled and there is essentially just one tier

- Some argue that we need a second tier consisting of non-lawyers certified to also do the law

- Acrimonious debates covering the benefits versus risks of a two-tiered approach are plentiful

- Coming down the road will be the potential of a third-tier consisting of Artificial Intelligence (AI)

- Questions abound about the tiers and the (shocking) chance of collapsing back into one tier

Introduction

Are two heads better than one?

What about three heads, are they even better still?

A rather fractious debate is taking place these days about the practice of law, and it involves a potential splintering of who or what can partake in proffering bona fide legal advice. Right now, it can be relatively successfully argued that there is really just one head, a solitary and tightly controlled possession, as it were, and meanwhile, some are advocating for a second head, while few are of the realization that a (surprising) third one is soon emerging too.

That might all seem somewhat mysterious, so let's unpack the matter.

There is an ongoing and intense debate about whether non-lawyers might potentially be permitted to practice law. Arguments are made that doing so would presumably increase access to justice and spur a justice-for-all aspiration, while fervent counter-arguments are made that the public would be subjected to a lesser capacity of legal representation and consequently experience a palpably diminished version of justice.

If non-lawyers were widely enabled and licensed to directly perform legal services and provide legal advice, it is said that a two-tiered approach to our entire means of justice would inexorably and inevitably arise, cleaving our courts and our judicial matters. There would ostensibly emerge a two-tiered version of our legal world, one represented by lawyers and the other being represented by non-lawyers, hewing into unequal halves the entire sense of adjudication and how our laws are applied.

I'm not going to wade per se into that voracious and acrimonious dispute, but, meanwhile, proffer that the two-tiered vision could actually become a three-tiered legal world. This is a surprising notion for many and for which few are giving any focused attention; albeit, rightfully so, instead of aiming their attention at the nearer term reality of a two-tier cleaving and less concerned or even cognizant about a potential futuristic third tier.

The Three Tiers Unveiled

What is the postulated third tier?

Some assert that the advent of Artificial Intelligence (AI) as a form of autonomous legal reasoning could be considered another layer or tier in our approach to justice.

In short, three options might emerge:

- Tier 1: Representation by a conventionally licensed attorney

- Tier 2: Representation by non-lawyer (a new type of licensing)

- Tier 3: Representation by AI legal reasoning (a new type of licensing)

This third rail, embodying advanced automation that verges onto the practice of law, already has been a focus of discussion and debate for many years. Notably, this arose precipitously due to the emergence of Internet-accessible online services such as LegalZoom and other such providers.

At first, making available static fill-in forms online that were legally oriented was not especially controversial, but this becomes a more pronounced controversy once the static became the dynamic, consisting of computer programs guiding how to fill in the forms and professing how to make use of them. The accepted custom of publishing legal forms and books containing legal artifacts became outstretched. Now, in more modern times, an active and proactive computer program was suddenly and seemingly dispensing a variant of "legal advice" (depending upon the definition of legal advice that one chooses to use).

As an aside, intense debates and unresolved disputes about the foundational meaning of "legal advice" remain open-ended and at issue. In that sense, it is an additional debate embedded within the debate about the licensing of lawyers versus non-lawyers.

There have been formalized attempts to definitively stipulate item-by-item what "legal advice" distinctly consists of, while others are apt to contend that legal advice is simply that which licensed attorneys to do in the course of their legal efforts. This latter way of defining "legal advice" is said by some to be circular and self-serving, since it would seem to enforce that by-definition alone, the only possible tier for the practice of law is ergo exclusively that of duly licensed attorneys.

The New Third Tier Handwringing

One viewpoint on these matters is that any substantive attempts to keep at bay the third tier will be fruitless and futile.

Here's the logic for this belief.

As AI gets more proficient at legal reasoning, such AI capabilities are going to be made available online, everywhere, and from anywhere. Thus, suppose that the United States legal establishment and government opt to ignore or otherwise cast aside the possible use of AI for providing legal advice, there are going to be those outside the purview of the U.S. that will undoubtedly make available such online services anyway. The allure of providing AI-powered legal services to make a buck will be immensely attractive and will spring forth like a vast field of blossoming tulips and daisies.

Presumably, U.S. citizens will be tempted to rely upon this "other world" online array of AI-powered legal advisory systems. Although those AI systems might be considered as outcasts or undesirables by those within the U.S. legal profession, it would seem that the public is undoubtedly going to flow toward the ease-of-use and potentially less-costly means of getting legal advice than resorting to human lawyers.

There is another stoking part of the contention that further bolsters this third-tier sustenance.

It would seem likely that lawyers themselves might also leverage those AI-powered legal reasoning capabilities, doing so to get a "second opinion" or readily get a double-check of their legal labors. If the lawyers are doing so, it would add encouragement to the makers of the AI-powered legal reasoning systems and therefore further fuel the expansion of those AI systems. In that sense, the legal profession itself will ironically spur the very thing that apparently is being sought to be closed down or excommunicated.

And, piling more kindling onto that fire, the pronouncements to have non-lawyers be allowed to practice law will be strengthened by those AI-powered legal reasoning systems. Non-lawyers can assert that they can proficiently practice law due to utilizing the AI-powered legal reasoning systems acting as an over-the-shoulder guide and legal mentor to them in their nascent legal toils.

There is a bit of a vicious cycle involved.

The better the AI becomes at legal reasoning, the more pressure brought to existing lawyers to leverage those capabilities, and the added pressure by non-lawyers to be permitted to practice law via their leveraging those capabilities too.

You could say that the third tier will boost the legitimacy and establishment of the second tier. In that case, the three-tier structure is overall reinforced and inspired toward formulation.

Ultimately, though, it could be that the "middle man" or "middle woman" is cut out of the picture entirely, such that neither a human lawyer and nor a human non-lawyer will be needed, reducing the three tiers back down to one-tier. That one tier would be the exclusive realm of the AI-powered legal reasoning systems. The revelation is that the third tier aided and abetted the formation of the second tier, and then eventually ate both of those two tiers (as in the assertion that *software eats the world*).

For existing lawyers, this last point of a collapsed one-tier consisting solely of AI legal reasoning systems is exceedingly farfetched since it is highly unlikely that within their lifetimes such AI capabilities will be borne out. Meanwhile, newbie students just now entering into law schools are perhaps somewhat prone to later on feeling some of this effervescence, but even they are unlikely to be around when AI gets to that veritable pinnacle (some would argue that it won't ever do so).

Conclusion

Do not though interpret these prognostic remarks as indicating that it is okay to put one's head-in-the-sand and hide from the progressive advances of AI for legal reasoning. That would most certainly be a mistake. Keep in mind that there is going to be a gradual advancement of AI legal reasoning and this will subtly and incessantly bear upon the debate about the lawyers versus non-lawyers' two-tiered world. As such, thinking about a proposed third tier, admittedly perhaps somewhat early on in its evolution, nonetheless provides important insights and is substantively worthwhile to contemplate.

We of course shouldn't get ahead of ourselves, yet nor do we want to be falling behind and get caught asleep at the legal wheel.

Note: *For supplemental materials depicting the aspects discussed in this chapter, refer to Appendix B, which contains various augmented diagrams, charts, and additional related facets of relevance.*

CHAPTER 11

AI & LAW:

TURING TEST

Key briefing points about this article:

- There isn't any AI yet today that is sentient and nor reaches the level of full human intelligence

- Nonetheless, there might someday be such vaunted AI and we'll need to know that it exists

- Within the AI field, there is a type of famous test for this known as the Turing Test

- It makes sense to recast the Turing Test into the field of law as it relates to AI and the law

- Once there is AI-enabled autonomous legal reasoning we'll want to validate its capabilities

Introduction

Did a human compose this sentence or did a computer do so?

Nowadays, it can be hard to readily discern whether something that you see or hear might be generated via a computer versus by the direct hand of a human.

That being said, computers that embody the latest in Artificial Intelligence (AI) are still not sentient, not even close, and do not be fooled or misled otherwise. Someday, presumably, it is assumed that AI will indeed be either sentient or possibly achieve a semblance of human intelligence, though one of the biggest questions will be the simplest of them all, namely, how will we know when such AI has been produced?

Your first thought might be that it seems blatantly obvious that we'll undoubtedly and instantly recognize when AI has achieved human-levels of intelligence. Along those lines, perhaps you are contemplating a notion that we'll know it when we witness it.

And with that helpful preamble, let's unpack the matter and take a closer look to try and figure out this conundrum.

When Is The There There

They say that beauty is in the eye of the beholder.

That might be true, but it is confoundingly problematic if you were to try and use that definition in a legal matter. In a sense, beauty would be relatively amorphous, semantically indeterminate, and be imbued with individualistic arbitrariness.

What else has those same qualms?

You might recall the famous utterance in 1964 by Supreme Court Justice Potter Stewart in the Jacobellis v Ohio case on obscenity, in which he indicated this about how to discern that which is hard-core pornography: "I shall not today attempt further to define the kinds of material I understand to be embraced within that shorthand description, and perhaps I could never succeed in intelligibly doing so. But I know it when I see it, and the motion picture involved in this case is not that."

This became known as the "I know it when I see it" test.

One could reasonably assert that the now-legendary phrase of "I know it when I see it" is in the same camp as the "eye of the beholder" refrain, once again be susceptible to individual arbitrariness and incurring other challenging woes as a means to definitively ascertain such matters.

Let's toss in an additional popular phrase into this word-salad mix.

You might be unfamiliar with the poetry of James Whitcomb Riley from the late 1800s, but you surely know the variants of his especially memorable poetic line: "When I see a bird that walks like a duck and swims like a duck and quacks like a duck, I call that bird a duck." Today's equivalent catchphrase is typically along the lines of if it walks like a duck and quacks like a duck, then it most probably is a duck.

Okay, so what does all of this add-up to and why does any of this make a difference?

Here's why this is a weighty and quite crucial matter: *It has to do with Artificial Intelligence (AI) and the law.*

First, let's start with the AI part of that equation and then bring back into view the law part of it.

A longstanding and vexing issue in the realm of AI has been the question of when we will know that we have successfully arrived at the sought-for destination. In this case, the destination presumably consisting of being able to craft a machine or computer-based system that can fully and truly embody or exhibit human intelligence.

Ponder this puzzling aspect for a moment and try to identify what techniques or methods you would use to ascertain that a computer with AI running on it has become equal to human intelligence (or, possibly even surpassed human intelligence, progressing beyond the mortal sphere and entering into the uncharted waters of superhuman intelligence).

Would you give the AI a copy of the SAT or ACT college entrance exam and use that as your indicator of it having reached the instantiation of human intelligence, presumably asking the AI to try and answer all of the posed test questions and then see what it says?

This might be an interesting way to get things started on the path toward assessing human intelligence embodiment, but I believe we would all likely agree that it is not especially satisfying and certainly not a complete form of testing.

Indeed, suppose that I cleverly decided to craft an AI system that was exclusively focused on passing the SAT or ACT tests, using various narrow-AI technologies, and pretty much programmed the computer to specifically be adept at those particular tests. If you then opted to have the AI take the SAT or ACT tests, and it passed with flying colors, would it be fair and reasonable to declare that AI has fully been achieved? I dare say, no, it would not be, and in a manner of speaking, the AI-existence test that was being used was faulty because it could too easily be fooled or otherwise be passed without striking at the heart of what AI is supposed to be.

Time to tie this all together into a tidy bow, using the opening remarks about commonplace word-salads.

You might argue that *you'll know it when you see it*, in terms of whether a computer has fully become AI-powered. Furthermore, if the computer can talk like a human, act like a human, and seem to think like a human, by gosh it most probably is true AI (this is a variant of the duck test, one might so suggest). Unfortunately, these clichés merely get us mired into the same muck of individual arbitrariness and does little to overcome those misfortunes.

There is a way to shift those sentiments into something that does have sharper teeth.

It turns out that insiders within the AI field have already come up with a type of test, or more akin to a structure or template of a test, known as the Turing Test.

Unfolding The Turing Test

Created by and named for the esteemed mathematician Alan Turing, he originally proposed in 1950 a means of testing AI that he described as an imitation game and it has stood the test of time, as it were, still highly regarded and cited in today's modern times.

The Turing Test or imitation game that he devised consists of a person that takes on the role of conducting an interrogation, asking questions of two subjects or participants, one being a human and the other being an AI system (neither of the two is directly seen by the interrogator). Imagine that the two subjects are hidden behind a curtain on a stage and that the interrogator can only interact indirectly via speaking or writing a message to them but cannot see them directly. This hiding of the subjects aids in what otherwise would be a rather perfunctory exercise of merely looking at the participants and visually ascertaining which is the human and which is the machine (assuming that the machine is not a robot fashioned to look identically like a human).

The interrogator does not know beforehand which of the two is the human and nor which of the two is the AI. For sake of convenience, label one of them as X and the other as Y. The interrogator asks questions or makes queries of the X and Y, and at some point, ascertains that the effort should be concluded. Upon so ending the effort, the interrogator is then to state whether X is the human or whether Y is the human, which alternatively could be stated by indicating whether X is the AI or whether Y is the AI.

The aim of the Turing Test is that if the interrogator is unable to differentiate between the two subjects, presumably the AI is thusly indistinguishable from the human, in terms of thinking, and thus we can conclude that the AI has achieved the equivalence of human intelligence. This greatly simplifies the seemingly intractable problem of trying to define what human intelligence consists of. If the AI can demonstrate intelligence to the same degree as a human, it can be said to be a thinking machine and have reached the aspirations of AI.

At a glance, this likely seems a handy way to solve this problem of

87

how to ascertain the achievement of AI. Please be aware though that there are various criticisms about the Turing Test, encompassing numerous limitations or weaknesses about it, and there is a slew of proffered suggestions about how to bolster or strengthen it.

In any case, consider how this then applies to AI and the law.

There are ongoing efforts to craft AI that can perform legal reasoning. It is believed that gradually, inexorably, these AI legal-beagle systems will be able to fully conduct legal reasoning and proffer legal advice, on par with that of human attorneys.

How will we know that the AI legal reasoning capabilities are sufficiently capable to practice law?

Aha, in many ways, this is the "I'll know it when I see it" potential malady, and, as such, perhaps the Turing Test could be reapplied to the context of the legal realm, entailing the use of the Turing Test to ascertain the legal proficiency and legal acumen of an AI system.

Conclusion

As additional food for thought, and for which it might make some crazed, if we are presumably going to eventually have AI that embodies human intelligence, we might readily assume that this AI could also become an attorney or lawyer, doing so in the same manner that a human with human intelligence can do so. The AI would study the law, perhaps be subject to taking a bar exam, and then upon doing so be considered the equivalent of a licensed attorney.

Not everyone is keen on the idea, some insist it won't ever be allowed to happen, whilst others sleep soundly at night by assuming that no AI will ever be able to cross that lofty threshold.

Note: *For supplemental materials depicting the aspects discussed in this chapter, refer to Appendix B, which contains various augmented diagrams, charts, and additional related facets of relevance.*

CHAPTER 12

AI & LAW:

NEXT ERA OF LAW

Key briefing points about this essay:

- American history and American law are joined at the hip and are worth jointly studying

- Legal scholars suggest that there have been three major eras of the law in the U.S.

- The three eras are known as (1) Age of discovery, (2) Age of faith, and (3) Age of Anxiety

- Questions arise as to what the next and thus fourth era will be

- Among the hypothesized next eras is the possibility of AI in the law as a key ingredient

Introduction

Past, present, and the future. We need to make sure we mindfully assess the past, gleaning lessons learned, of which we can potentially leverage those identified insights into our present day, and meanwhile be accordingly making sharper plans for the future.

All of those suggestions apply to the history of the law. Indeed, American history is inextricably intertwined with the history of American law. Akin to two beams of light that seem to shimmer and travel in unison, anyone that seriously studies the law must also be cognizant of the coexistent historical context that precipitated changes in the law, and which inherently sparked new theories about law, along with ultimately spurring alterations in the practice of law.

Some assert that American law can be historically stratified into distinct eras. The most well-known stratification is undoubtedly exhibited in the research by legal scholar Grant Gilmore that proposed in the late 1970s that there have been three eras of American law. His work was based on an earlier postulated set of three eras by Karl Llewellyn in 1960, of which Gilmore then bolstered and expanded upon that initial framework.

What are the three hypothesized eras of American law?

The quick answer is that they are encapsulated by these monikers:

- *Age of Discovery* occurring from the 1800s until the Civil War

- *Age of Faith* occurring from the Civil War to WWI

- *Age of Anxiety* occurring from WWI to present (as of the 1970s)

Let's briefly unpack these three eras and then shift into a deeply beguiling question, namely, what is the next or presumably fourth era of American law?

Deep Dive Into The Three Eras

The first era was coined as the *Age of Discovery* and said to have occurred from the 1800s until the Civil War, throughout which there was an initial formulation of a legal edifice for America. This was based to a great extent on the reuse of English common law, inexorably being shorn into a stylized and substantive instantiation that would become uniquely American law.

The second era lasted from the Civil War until WWI and has been anointed as the *Age of Faith* (side note: in this context do not misconstrue the word "faith"; it has no bearing on any religious related matters and instead relies upon having a sense of faith in the law itself). During this era, there was a purported attempt to perceive and shape the law as a form of rigorous science, out of which there were presumably legal truths that could axiomatically be discovered and derived. It was said to be a time when one ought to have utter faith that the law was right and just since it was essentially scientifically provable as such.

The third era arose following WWI and is referred to as the *Age of Anxiety*. When Gilmore wrote about these eras in the 1970s, he indicated that the Age of Anxiety was still underway. Today, most legal scholars assert that the Age of Anxiety is still upon us (some exceptions will be mentioned in a moment herein). The anxiety was a sentiment being sparked as a realization that the prior assurance of faith in legal truths was mislaid and could no longer adequately serve as a foundational structure for understanding and maturation of the field of law.

Be aware that there is ongoing and at times acrimonious debate about all facets of these eras. For example, some suggest that the naming of the three eras is misstated or a mischaracterization of their meaning. Others assert that there have not been three eras per se and that it is some other number, perhaps a lesser number of eras or a larger count. Discourse also occurs entailing where to best cut or divide the historical periods for whichever eras might be propounded.

If you'll allow for a bit of levity on this potentially abstemious conundrum, one supposes that because those versed in the law are apt to be especially versed at legal argumentation, there is little surprise that there would be rancorous arguments about the nature and scope of any decreed eras of American law.

In any case, take at face value that there have been three eras and they have generally occurred in the time frames alleged.

Speculating About The Next Era

The logical questions naturally flowing from those three presumed eras consist of:

- What will be the fourth era?

- When will the fourth era begin (or has it already)?

- What is the basis for asserting there will be a fourth era?

- How will the fourth era be differentiated from the prior eras?

- And so on.

The bottom line is that there is no widespread consensus as to the answers to those questions.

This is a situation consisting of both good news and bad news. The good news is that there is a healthy dialogue occurring about the advent of a fourth era and what it portends. The bad news is that anyone seeking a clear-cut answer and a definitive proclamation about the fourth era will need to wait until that day arrives.

Consider some of the proposals regarding a postulated fourth era.

Research at the Columbia Law School has proposed that the fourth era should be coined as the Age of Consent. Their theory asserts that this is a new legal era that has already started to emerge and consists of the maximization of individual choice. Meanwhile, a competing proposal that depicts an era known as the Age of Information is proffered by the Northwestern University School of Law. In their view, we are increasingly being immersed in a fourth era inhabiting the abundance of information, giving rise to computable legal standards and dynamic legal rules (readers interested in this latter topic should refer to my Daily Journal posting of September 17, 2020, on the related discussion of legal micro-directives).

In my latest research on the legal eras, I've emphasized that whatever the fourth era is eventually discovered or declared to be, the odds are that Artificial Intelligence will come to play and be either a notable catalyst within the new era or might very well be the defining cornerstone for the era. To further clarify, it could be that there is a fourth era that arises separately and apart from the advent of AI, but for which will be demonstrably impacted by AI, and then it could be that a perhaps *fifth era* emerges that is shaped and borne directly from the advent of autonomous AI Legal Reasoning (AILR).

Conclusion

For those that might believe it folly or valueless to speculate about the next era (and its future ancestors), this kind of matter is actually of both a notable theoretical and practical significance.

By being able to anticipate the fourth era, we might collectively as a society and especially within the legal field be able to prepare accordingly for what is to come, along with the added potential of shaping or altering course if the emergent fourth era seems untoward or otherwise undesirable. For legal practitioners, knowing what the fourth era constitutes could aid significantly in their training and attention, and be a crucial harbinger of what the practice of law is coming to possibly become.

An eyes-wide-open perspective on the next era of American law certainly and indubitably seems to surpass a head-in-the-sand posture.

.

Note: *For supplemental materials depicting the aspects discussed in this chapter, refer to Appendix B, which contains various augmented diagrams, charts, and additional related facets of relevance.*

CHAPTER 13

AI & LAW:

PURE LOGIC INSUFFICIENCY

Key briefing points about this article:

- Some believe that we ought to be able to turn the law into a set of axiomatic logic

- Doing so would presumably make the law easily computerized and become widely accessible

- Logic-based law could theoretically enable computational legality determinations

- Ongoing attempts at using AI in this quest for a pure logic approach are underway

- Complexity ensues and there are pitfalls aplenty that still are to be resolved

Introduction

When people think wistfully or perhaps wishfully about the law, they often in an offhand manner characterize the law as though it ought to be entirely axiomatic.

In short, the notion is that since the law is seemingly written down, and since it appears to entail some semblance of logic, ergo the most obvious and natural way to try and computerize the law would be to compose it into a series of logic-based statements. The resulting axiomatic system would presumably be easy to run and maintain, thus, obviating all the messiness of today's wrangling with the paper-based and narrative heavy-laden nature of the law.

Indeed, during my classes on Artificial Intelligence (AI) and the law, one of the questions I most often get asked involves the seemingly apparent notion that pure logic ought to be able to encapsulate the law.

In essence, rather than dealing with all of the various AI-empowered and profusely complex systems techniques and advanced computer-based technologies, just simply put the law into an everyday logic formulation. All we have to do is perhaps state that A leads to B, and B leads to C, and thus proceed to encode the law into a rudimentary series of logic-based statements and rules. No-fuss, no muss. Life would be a lot easier if this could be undertaken.

Imagine a large corpus of all the laws transformed into a set of pristine logic-based assertions. Whenever a legal case arose, you would log in to this mighty database, enter in the particulars of your case, and voila, the system would churn through possibly thousands upon thousands of logic rules and spit out your outcome.

What a wonderful life it would be.

Does Logic Cut The Bill

Well, not everyone views this as a great wonderment.

The classic concern is that these rules might be so voluminous and interconnected that the legal result generated is either an oddball result or does not lend itself to any readily understood semblance of logic. This seems counterintuitive that something based entirely on resolute logic could somehow not be logically understood by us.

Potentially, this confounding facet could arise if the logic is so intertwined and convoluted to the degree that (let's say) a printout might run for hundreds of pages showing all the logic enacted occurrences. Presumably, this vastness of enacted rules would be beguiling for anyone to comprehensively make heads nor tails of what the underlying logic readily comports.

In a forest-for-the-trees kind of aspect, we might lose sight of a greater cohesiveness of the law by having it codified into those zillions of itsy-bitsy immaculate rules.

Another concern is that the rules themselves might be suspect. Suppose that a nefarious rule got embedded into this morass of logic-based legal theorems and stipulations (being surreptitiously implanted or having been added on the up-and-up but having unanticipated adverse consequences). Who determines which rules belong and which do not? How could we ferret out the rules that are ominous or untoward? Indeed, think of the ongoing effort required to maintain and do the upkeep on this outsized and overwhelmingly massive collection of rules about the law.

Well, be aware, a robust counterargument to those contentions is that we already do roughly the same thing, though it is primarily paper-based, crudely undertaken by hand, and presumably just as much a quagmire as if it were inside an overarching computerized database. By putting the entirety of the law into some set of sharply delineated online rules, at least we would have a better chance at using the same computer-based proclivities to scan for foul rules and otherwise manage the rules and therefore better manage the nature of our laws.

Round and round we go, whereby there are arguments to be made that it would behoove us to seek and craft this logic-based law codification vision versus those that decry such an approach as leading us down a heartless path and possibly letting machines be our ultimate ruler.

But The Feasibility You Say

Let's take a step back from all of that thunder and lightning and ask a simpler question, namely, whether such a large-scale logic-encapsulating system is feasible, to begin with.

The base assumption underlying the aforementioned debate is that we could in fact create a crisp computer-based logic-running system to house the transmuted semantically indeterminate laws. One supposes that if we can get mankind to the moon, surely, we could devise an online system to embody and enact the laws of the land.

Sorry, it is not as easy as you might think.

There are plenty of research efforts underway to try and reach this legal-rules nirvana, though to-date the journey has been stymied in many respects.

A popular logic-encoding programming language typically used in a legal context is called ASP (Answer Set Programming). Many of the efforts toward turning law into code are oftentimes undertaken via the use of ASP. It is considered a declarative programming language, which differs from the usual procedural oriented programming languages that you might have toyed with while taking a computer programming course in college or online.

A declarative approach means that you can list the rules and do so without worrying about the order in which they are to be utilized.

Normally, when writing a program in a conventional procedural language, you need to specify the sequence of which line is to be performed one after another. Not so in a declarative language. Instead, you can pretty much toss the rules into a collection and then let the system sort through the ordering that will be needed to appropriately utilize the rules. This spares the developer from having to meticulously figure out any sequencing aspects. Besides ASP, other relatively popular declarative programming languages used for legal encoding include ASPIC+, Prolog, and others.

Non-Monotonic Reasoning

One tricky conundrum for the use of straight-ahead logic is that you almost always need to contend with what is referred to as non-monotonic logical reasoning. This might not have been covered in your math classes or it maybe has been a while since you've studied such matters. Let's start by quickly defining monotonic reasoning, which is the notion that logical conclusions can be attained and are soundly concludable even if a new clause or rule is later added into the set. On the other hand, non-monotonic reasoning has provisions for having newly added rules that might invalidate prior reached conclusions.

That's a mouthful.

The Tweety Bird example is a favorite among most explanations on this difference between monotonic and non-monotonic reasoning. Tweety Bird, the one in the Looney Tunes cartoons, provides handy fodder for easily elucidating the matter. Suppose that we agree that Tweety is a bird. Hopefully, this assertion does not raise any hackles or immediate discord, but if it does, please go along with me for the moment anyway.

Next, suppose it is asserted that birds fly. We seem to then be able to reach a quite sensible and logic-based conclusion that Tweety can fly since we know Tweety is a bird and we also now know that birds fly. Ergo, we'll include into the legal corpus that a conclusion has been reached that Tweety can fly.

At some later point in time, there are additional rules added into the database, including that Tweety is a penguin, and then later after that insertion, there is this rule added: Penguins cannot fly. Oops, that seems to be a problem. Earlier, it was concluded that Tweety could fly, but now, based on Tweety being a penguin and the added facet that penguins cannot fly, we have to (presumably) recant the earlier arrived at conclusion.

A monotonic form of logical reasoning won't let you undo that prior conclusion, while a non-monotonic structure would allow the new conclusion to essentially override or somehow cope with the conflicting prior conclusion.

Before you get irked that this might all seem like a trivial matter, think about court cases that led to judgments and that became the understanding or meaning of the law, and then, later on, some other judgment countered or overruled the earlier ruling. It turns out that if you have a set of thousands upon thousands of logic-based rules, and you allow for a non-monotonic world, the repercussions are quite explosive in terms of having to then contend with all the rippling and cascading effects that such a later-on new ruling can have.

There are catchy names for this logic-based phenomenon, known sometimes as skeptical reasoning, credulous reasoning, zombie-arguments, and so on. Dealing with non-monotonic reasoning consideration is puzzling mathematically and can be computationally hard or intractable. Nonetheless, despite the problems it introduces, I think we can all likely concur that the real-world cannot be cast in monotonic reasoning and we must find viable means to employ non-monotonic reasoning.

Conclusion

All told, there is a slew of issues and problems facing the attempts to codify the law into what might be characterized as pure logic. Fortunately, there are abundant and diligently concerted efforts going on to do so. Note that others believe that it might be a kind of dead-end and thus other forms of AI-reasoning techniques and technologies will be required to shift the law into being computationally usable or reasoned.

Or, it could be that we discover a mixture of the two is the best overall approach.

Anyone that was to summarily conclude right now that one way is the right way, could subsequently find themselves facing down the cannon of the monotonic form of logic and be clamoring for a non-monotonic viewpoint when or if their acrimonious contention turned out to be untrue.

That's the way of logic.

Note: *For supplemental materials depicting the aspects discussed in this chapter, refer to Appendix B, which contains various augmented diagrams, charts, and additional related facets of relevance.*

Dr. Lance B. Eliot

CHAPTER 14

AI & LAW:
LEGAL SIMPLIFICATION

Key briefing points about this essay:

- An ongoing drumbeat is whether the laws are overly convoluted and need to be simplified

- Simplifying the laws might provide upsized benefits for the public and the practice of law

- Not everyone is convinced that law simplification is an answer and might worsen matters

- AI has the potential for providing a type of legal simplification engine

- There are qualms that the AI simplifying machinations could bode for legal difficulties

Introduction

There is an ongoing tension between the law as necessarily being complex and unwieldy, perhaps innately so, versus the belief that the law can inexorably be greatly simplified and streamlined.

The public at large would presumably be more amenable to observing the laws if the arcane morass of the laws were straight-and-narrow rather than existent as bloated and altogether confounding. In theory, the courts too would be better off, and the practice of law might be less obtuse were it not for the existing oblique nature of our laws.

Not everyone though might hold that same view of seeking heightened simplicity. Recall the famous words of Montesquieu (1748) as uttered in De l'Esprit des Lois: "Thus when a man takes on absolute power, he first thinks of simplifying the law. In such a state one begins to be more affected by technicalities than by the freedom of the people, about which one no longer cares at all."

In the quote by Montesquieu, there is a raised concern of an authoritarian state taking on absolute power and opting to subsequently simplify the law. This simplification, in turn, might lead to law that no longer affords the freedoms that we enjoy and could become stagnant and stifling in their effects.

Depending upon how one wishes to interpret the matter, it is plausible to argue that the pursuit of simplicity in itself is not necessarily a best-fit aspiration and nor always proffers a beneficial outcome. That's not to denigrate the value of simplicity and only to offer food for thought that we cannot assume axiomatically that if laws were simpler it ergo portends that we would be better off. What could presumably be said, at the very least, is that the law is simpler than it once was.

There is also the matter of the chicken versus the egg in this conundrum.

Perhaps Montesquieu is merely pointing out that those wishing to ultimately take control will tend toward simplifying the law, greasing their devious and strident efforts to overtake society and summarily dictate the nature of our laws. The notion of simplicity is inadvertently drawn into this maneuvering of power tectonic shifts and otherwise is a standalone topic that unfairly is being dragged through the mud.

In a sense, simplicity has nothing or little to do with the power dynamics per se, neither promoting it and nor inhibiting it and merely an unsuspecting tool for (in this instance) untoward ends.

Questions also arise at the endpoint of this quest for simplicity. In essence, can one continue to split the atom indefinitely, or is there a stopping point at which the reach of simplicity can go no further? In the use case of the law, the simplest linguistic utterance might be elusive and indeterminate. Endless debates about trying to squeeze more blood from a rock, aiming to make the laws simpler and simpler, could be distracting and unwieldy of themselves.

Practitioners might find this discourse on the simplicity versus the complexity of the law as rather philosophical and less so applied or valued in the actual practice of law.

AI And The Simplification Engine

Let's shift gears and toss the advent of Artificial Intelligence (AI) and the law into the mix to see if we can get some grounded traction on the matter.

One belief is that the use of AI will inevitably simplify the law.

Here's how.

It is customarily assumed that to achieve any true semblance of AI and the law, the use of AI techniques and technologies such as Machine Learning (ML) and Deep Learning (DL) would need to scan the text of our laws and pattern-match at the lowest level of tokenization. This would likely need to be augmented by human lawyers that aid in the labeling of these minimalist linguistic participials and provide by hand guidance for the ML/DL during those AI "learning" efforts.

Inexorably, this mechanization would produce simpler and simpler laws or at least AI-embodied laws that were transmuted from our everyday present laws.

If we then began to utilize the AI to provide legal reasoning and aid in judicial matters, a type of slippery slope will then have been intrinsically traversed. The now inner coded simpler variants of the laws by the AI would become the de facto set of laws. Eventually, there would seem to be little need for and nor reliance upon the laws on the books, as it were, and instead the AI-based and derived simpler laws would rue the day.

Thus, we fed into the AI the existent arcane and complicated laws, and out pops the simpler codified set. Voila, while trying to achieve artificially intelligent systems for use as automated and autonomous lawyers, judges, and the like, we just so happened to hit two birds with one stone, having generated simpler laws in the same breath.

Okay, based on that scenario, we will ultimately then land upon the shores of simpler laws.

Is that a good thing or a bad thing?

Well, for those asserting that simpler is always better, this must be a good thing. We got lucky, some would say, achieving a twofer by hence having AI for autonomous legal reasoning and simultaneously transformed the byzantine present-day laws into a simpler collective that is available on-line at any time from any location on the planet.

What's not to like about this, they would exhort.

Consider some of the counter-arguments.

If the laws of today were divided and subdivided into simpler pieces, being churned through in a sausage factory manner, the voluminous nature would worsen and make it even harder for lawyers to practice law. Presumably, human attorneys would not seemingly be able to keep mentally attune to the millions upon millions of such simplified laws that might be so derived.

In that sense, whereas it might appear that the law is being simplified, the reality would be that it is becoming increasingly complex by a classic forest-for-the-trees kind of difficulty (more and more trees obscuring the overarching shape of the forest).

Imagine too the permutations and explosive combinations that could arise.

Each of the itsy-bitsy laws is undoubtedly going to be related to many others of the same ilk. A particular simplified law might find itself interconnected with dozens of others of these simplifications, or more likely to hundreds, thousands, or millions of them. As a crude analogy, it is said that the human brain has about 100 billion neurons, which is certainly a large number. That being said, the estimates are that there are perhaps 100 trillion interconnections. The number of interconnections is many times that of the actual number of neurons, and indeed it is generally believed that the basis for our mental prowess is as much due to the interconnections as much as it is due to the neurons themselves.

All told, the viewpoint about AI and the law by some is that if indeed this simpler mantra is going to be the core foundation for how autonomous AI-based legal reasoning will be achieved, we might be opening up a Pandora's box and not even realize that we are doing so.

Per any topic that falls within the realm of the law, please know that there are cantankerously extensive debates on this topic and numerous points and counterpoints of the prophesized Dystopian result. For example, it could be the exact opposite of the aforementioned computational rendering, such that the AI embodiment converts the laws into inherently complex magnums and does not generate the simplifications that some assume will arise. In that case, if you believe that complexity is our friend, we would be thankful for the AI providing such a mechanism.

Conclusion

Yet another perspective is that it won't matter whether the AI serves as a grist mill and turns laws into being simpler or more complex since we humans won't care. We'll treat the AI as a veritable black box, having it undertake all of our legal wranglings. No more human lawyers or human judges. Just the AI. We'll be satisfied with whatever internal makes-the-hamburgers kind of intricacies exists, not being interested in looking under-the-hood.

That seems a bit farfetched and indubitably would spark Montesquieu, if alive today, toward worrying that the AI might undertake absolute power and, as we all know, lead to absolute corruption (per the wise words of Lord John Emerich Edward Dalberg-Acton).

.

Note: *For supplemental materials depicting the aspects discussed in this chapter, refer to Appendix B, which contains various augmented diagrams, charts, and additional related facets of relevance.*

CHAPTER 15

AI & LAW:
DUALISM WITH MORALITY

Key briefing points about this essay:

- The law has a close cousin, morality, for which there is at times agreement and sometimes not

- Society has wrestled with the dualism of the law and morality for millennia

- Recent advances in AI have led to attempts at embedding AI-enabled moral agents into software

- Likewise, there is a need to embed AI-enabled law-oriented agents into software

- Inevitably these two types of AI agencies will clash and the question of resolution is still open

Introduction

Two peas in a pod. Except that sometimes there is only one pea in the pod and the other one is left out altogether.

What am I referring to?

The focus herein entails the crucial roles that both the law and the tenets of morality undertake in our overall socio-economic and legal world. As will be discussed, advances in technology via the use of Artificial Intelligence (AI) are quickly gaining ground in terms of embodying morality oriented facets into everyday computer applications, sometimes referred to as MoralTech, and meanwhile, there is increasingly widespread use of LegalTech that encompasses embedding law-stipulating AI-agents into complex software systems.

Let's begin this discussion with the fundamentals of how the law and morality are at times fully aligned and at other times are utterly opposed to each other, and then ease into the auspicious notion of having AI-powered law-oriented agency and moral-oriented agency.

The Fundamentals Of Law And Morality

Some perceive that the law and morality are inextricably intertwined, being at times fully compatible with each other while at other times regrettably acting as bickering foes.

The tension between the law and the doctrines of morality can be traced to (at least) the days of Plato. Of course, you don't need to go back that far in time to get mired in the morass of where the laws begin and end, and where morality begins and ends, therein.

Legal scholars have repeatedly exhorted that there is a conundrum involving laws that permit an act that would otherwise be considered as immoral, and meanwhile also legally bans certain acts that are either morally permissible or possibly even considered as morally obligatory.

Morality might be hidden within the laws and not be immediately apparent to the eye.

Some assert that morality is found more so within the *shadow of the law*, consisting of those facets not directly stated in the law that nonetheless we associate with the law. It is said that the law casts a large shadow for which many of the acts that we are bound to either undertake or avoid are not explicitly stated per se in the laws and instead are presumed to be implied by various semantic overlay and open-ended moral interpretation.

Things are indubitably rough on the public at large when there is a conflict between what the law states and what morality seems to dictate. A salient remark in the famous legal treatise entitled *The Law* by Frederic Bastiat in 1850 illuminates vividly this grueling point: "When law and morality contradict each other, the citizen has the cruel alternative of either losing his [her] moral sense or losing his [her] respect for the law."

You can find two diametrically opposed perspectives on what to do about any contradictions between the law and morality. Some fervently insist that the laws are the laws, and nobody is above the law, even if they are wanting to claim that they imbue some morality or moral code that rightfully takes them outside the law. On the other side of that coin are the arguments that whenever legality and morality butt heads, legality shall be the loser, and unquestionably by the adamant and abundant degree it is morality that must be upheld.

As they say, be wary of the web that we weave when trying to straighten out the moments when law and morality are not well aligned.

AI Enters Into The Picture

This is all quite interesting and at times perhaps vague and unspecified, but it becomes an even greater challenge as we head toward a future consisting of Artificial Intelligence (AI) and the law. In a sense, the rubber is about to meet the road.

How so?

There is an increasing hue and cry that AI systems are being fostered into this world and for which those AI mechanizations are violating at times various vital ethical principles. For example, consider the use case of an AI-enabled application that decides who will be granted a home loan or a car loan. Via the use of today's advances in Machine Learning (ML) and Deep Learning (DL) techniques and technologies, an AI system is crafted that can quickly assess the applications submitted for a loan. By eschewing the normal laborious effort incurred via human loan assessors, the AI can perform the evaluations faster, more consistently, and without the vagaries or foibles that the human evaluators possess.

But then again, maybe not all is so readily tried and true.

It turns out that sometimes these AI systems using ML/DL are landing into a rather forbidden territory. Keep in mind that Machine Learning and Deep Learning are nothing more than computational pattern matching algorithms that mathematically analyze data to find identifiable patterns. They are not sentiment AI and nor do we have as yet any semblance of such sentience. Indeed, there isn't any common-sense reasoning embodied within the current AI.

This makes a difference in that the AI-powered loan processing system can readily land upon a computationally "satisfying" pattern that is based on race or perhaps gender (satisfying means, in this context, that it offers a statistically substantive approach, regardless of the societal implications). Those that have developed the AI might not readily be able to ferret out how the AI is deciding upon the loan applications. As such, the AI might proceed along, doing so for thousands upon thousands of loan applications, perhaps in the millions of applicants, with nobody realizing how the loan selection is being rendered.

One of the growing concerns about AI ML/DL is that it tends to lack any kind of transparency and only provides mathematically arcane indications that defy logically sensible explanations.

An effort to cope with these matters involves having companies adopt a set of AI Ethics principles to govern how they build AI systems and how they select AI systems for licensing or acquisition. Assuming that the adopters of the AI Ethics precepts abide by the stated conditions, presumably, there will be a lower likelihood of AI systems that violate ethical or moral stipulations.

What some seem to be neglecting or overlooking is the need to equally ensure that the AI is legally abiding by the laws.

In short, the expectation must be that the AI is <u>both</u> lawful and morally above board.

A recent trend involves implanting into AI systems a component for the ethics or morals side of the matter. Imagine a loan granting AI system that is keeping track of loan approvals and loan rejections, and then detects by itself that perhaps there is an internal bias shaping the choices, ascertaining that the use of race or gender is occurring (for example). The AI would then attempt to alert to such a malady or might seek to self-heal itself, adjusting how it is making the decisions and aim to eliminate the reliance upon those biased factors.

The Disagreement Dilemma Rears Its Head

This brings us to the moment of keen intrigue herein.

Suppose the AI has such an embedded morality component or so-called *agent* (the accepted parlance in the AI field is to refer to AI entities oftentimes as "agents") and also has another component that focuses on the legal or lawful agency aspects. Two such agents are working in real-time, one that is assessing the moral or ethical ramifications of the AI, and the other evaluating and attempting to regulate the legal facets.

Here's the million-dollar question, as it were: *What happens when the embedded moral agent and the embedded legal agent emit differing assessments that are entirely opposed in terms of what the AI ought to be doing (or ought to not be doing)?*

For sure, this is a hefty quandary and mirrors the same points made earlier about the arduous and insidious issues that arise when the law and morality clash. To date, this ugly problem has not been especially apparent within AI since so few AI systems have these embedded components. Also, realize too that if the AI has only one such component, perhaps the morality agent, it wins by default since it is the only agency within the AI, and likewise, if the legal agent is the only agency then it wins due to the lack of any counterbalancing morality agent.

My prediction is that we are going to gradually and inexorably become more aware of this problematic issue and will need to put in place practical and usable ways to deal with it.

Conclusion

All told, trying to get automation to resolve conflicts between the law and morality is beyond the pay grade of current AI. Nonetheless, we can and should expect the AI to be able to detect when such disputes arise and can partake in limited and focused conflict resolution efforts, doing so within predetermined boundaries.

Meanwhile, society as a whole is undeniably going to wrestle with seemingly intractable disagreements between the law and morality, doing so presumably for a long time, possibly forever, and for which even if Plato were alive today could not be readily and fully resolved.

.

———

Note: *For supplemental materials depicting the aspects discussed in this chapter, refer to Appendix B, which contains various augmented diagrams, charts, and additional related facets of relevance.*

CHAPTER 16

AI & LAW:
LEGAL DEFINITIONS OF AI

Key briefing points about this essay:

- Definitions are the lifeblood of the law and inextricably the practice of law too

- Many a court case has hinged precariously on the definition of this word or that phrase

- Meanwhile, consider that AI is gradually and inexorably coming into the field of law

- And yet there is ample ambiguity about what "AI" entails and definitions of AI are aplenty

- This gives rise to examining a definition of AI as codified into the National Defense Act

Introduction

Any budding attorney learns pretty quickly that definitions can make or break your day. Whether examining a recently passed piece of legislation or perhaps giving a contract some close inspection, the importance of definitions arises with near certainty.

Is the terminology well-specified or is it sloppy and proffers numerous loopholes? Are the crucial words and phrases carefully defined or are they used with abandon and seem vacuous?

In contrast to the average person, lawyers know well the importance of definitions. Many a court case has hinged on the definition of a particular word or phrase. Tremendous legal battles have been waged as a result of arguments over the meaning of the tiniest of words.

Even the general public is likely aware of the now-classic debate over the word "is" when Bill Clinton during his presidency stated that "There's nothing going on between us" and then explained to a grand jury that "It depends on what the meaning of the word 'is' is." In this instance, the splitting of hairs dealt with whether the word "is" encapsulates the meaning of "was" or instead only meant the present tense and not the past.

Indubitably, definitions are crucial, and especially so in legal discourse.

Speaking of splitting hairs, another vital element about definitions entails what exactly the meaning of a "definition" itself entails. We all seem to accept the notion that a definition is that which defines something. This though is a bit recursive since it defines the word "definition" via the use of the word define, which might leave us meandering down a rabbit hole since we next need to stipulate the nature of the word "define" too.

Aristotle famously provided a definition of "definition" by indicating that it is a phrase that signifies a thing's essence. Notice that this definition, fortunately, does not contain a self-referential denotation and therefore would seem to proffer some modest progress on clarifying the matter. Per his wise wording, we seem to vaguely know that a definition can be or is presumed to be a phrase, and the phrase provides a telling about a thing, for which the portrayal is intended to strike the core or essence about that thing.

Some linguists and philosophers do not especially agree with Aristotle's indication. The angst involves the supposition that perhaps a definition is a kind of absolute. There is an implied sense that a definition is ironclad and abides by a law of nature such that it is inviolate and never changing. As such, the argument is that definitions are instead variable, ever-changing, and a social construct that merely reflects a type of crowdsourcing, namely that if enough people concur about a definition or even the definition of definition then that's what it is.

In short, there are no absolutes, only relative meanings.

This brings us back to the legal viewpoint underlying all of this discussion. In theory, supposing that definitions are purely relative, it means that there is always going to be room for argument about the meaning of something. This then opens the door to enabling legal disputes, since you can nearly always find a path toward undercutting a definition or try to argue for an alternative definition that presumably supports your side and undermines the opposing side.

Legal argumentation has a lot to do with making arguments involving definitions. If a definition in a case seems to be detrimental to your legal posture, you can attempt to challenge the definition and fervently attack it. Meanwhile, if a definition seems to be supportive of your position, you'll need to muster a strong defense to bolster and defend the definition.

A definition then is only as good as the strength of reasoning that keeps it intact.

There are ordinary definitions such as those found in the everyday dictionary and commonly used in ongoing societal affairs. For most lawyers, the definitions that really hit home are those that are statutory. For example, when a legislative body passes a law and includes various definitions, those become a kind of contract between the lawmakers and the people subject to those laws. The language specified is presumably laying a legal grounding and provides a semantic foundation for expressing what the law portends.

Definitions can be expressed by a concepts-oriented approach, depicting what a given word is supposed to mean, abstractly, and do so by offering a sentence or two to explain what it is all about. Another approach involves providing an example of what the word means. You can also try articulating the constituent parts or components that indicate the meaning. There is the approach of defining something by negation, stating what it is not, and therefore allow the reader to understand the word via knowing what it presumably must otherwise be. You can use enumeration. And so on.

This illuminates that there are multiple methods for composing or stating a definition, all of which have their own respective strengths and weaknesses, and for which a canny lawyer can leverage accordingly when disputing the definitions involved in a court case.

One would hope that a legislative body would be mindfully careful when providing definitions and attempt to make those definitions as bulletproof as possible. The more slippage or leeway within the definitions would suggest that the more ambiguous will be the results. How can people accede to what the law states if the law cannot deterministically and unambiguously clarify what the law presages?

Now that we've covered that muddy and rutty road about the maladies associated with definitions, let's turn our attention to a definition of increasing need and qualm.

Defining AI Is No Piece Of Cake

What is the definition of Artificial Intelligence (AI)?

I'm guessing that most have not given the topic much attention per se. You daily are bound to hear or read the AI moniker, oft used in blaring headlines, and merely take at face value that it has something to do with intelligence and something to do with being artificial. Perhaps the imagery of a robot comes to mind, or possibly you hark back to HAL in the movie *2001: A Space Odyssey,* and that is what your definition of AI embodies.

In Chapter 11, I discussed the meaning of AI as somewhat ascertained via the Turing Test, which involves a type of "I'll know it when I see it" method to defining AI. That avenue is not particularly satisfying when it comes to passing laws and establishing contracts, thus other approaches must be assuredly undertaken.

For an attorney, knowing the definition of AI might seem nothing more than an idle activity and pretty much inconsequential.

I dare say that the meaning of AI will gradually and inexorably have a tremendous import for lawyers, for the practice of law, and the nature of our courts and justice.

Here's why.

AI will be infused into the making of laws and the promulgation of laws. AI-based legal reasoning systems will partake in the performing of legal tasks, at times supplementing the acts of human lawyers and inevitably autonomously doing so. Ergo, being aware of and having an understanding of AI is tantamount to anticipating the future of being in the law and serving as an attorney.

Also, the chances are high that you'll begin to see AI emerging amidst the legal cases that you deal with.

For example, an attorney specializing in real estate is certainly going to eventually find themselves immersed in a legal case that has at issue an AI-based real estate system that perhaps led someone astray or make "judgments" that are at the question in the case. Overall, a modern-day attorney will ultimately see AI permeating all areas of legal life and therefore will have to recognize when such AI is at the heart of a case and how to contend with the AI injection thereof.

Yet another reason for a lawyer to be aware of the meaning of AI involves examining a newly passed law that explicitly identifies AI as a part of the legal wording of the regulation.

Or, maybe when aiding the crafting of a law or perhaps drafting a private contract, there will be a need to incorporate the notion of AI and therefore its definition therein too.

If none of that yet seems compelling about why having a definition of AI is significant, perhaps some added fuel to the fire might help.

There is ongoing and rancorous debate about whether AI ought to be somehow be decreed as having personhood, gaining a semblance of rights and privileges akin to that of humans. It would seem any attorney of any specialty would want to partake in such discussions, given the magnitude of the legal repercussions. The same can be said for thorny legal issues such as the liability associated with AI systems, the responsibilities of AI systems, and so on.

Returning then to the question about what is AI, or more definitively what is the definition of AI, some trace the earliest establishment to the efforts of Professor John McCarthy and his indication in a 1955 paper that said this: "For the present purpose the artificial intelligence problem is taken to be that of making a machine behave in ways that would be called intelligent if a human were so behaving." He also stated that AI is the matter of "getting a computer to do things which, when done by people, are said to involve intelligence."

Years later, in a 2007 paper, he defined AI this way: "It is the science and engineering of making intelligent machines, especially intelligent computer programs."

Those initial definitions are akin to what you would see in most dictionaries today and have generally stood the test of time. But if you take a closer look, you would realize that such a definition is wanting in many sorrowful ways. The shortness, ambiguity, and semantic flimsiness is nearly overwhelming and makes those definitions seemingly inoperable for any suitable legal purposes.

Exemplar Of AI As Defined In The Law

We therefore can turn out attention to definitions of AI that have been codified into the law.

Let's use the one such instance found in the *National Defense Authorization Act of Fiscal Year 2019* as an exemplar.

Within the portion labeled as *Division A: Department of Defense Authorizations*, and within it, the sub-portion labeled *Title II: Research, Development, Test, and Evaluation*, and within that the Subtitle B: *Program Requirements, Restrictions, and Limitations*, you would find this definition of AI as indicated in Section 238 of the passed bill:

SEC. 238. Joint Artificial Intelligence Research, Development, And Transition Activities.

(g) ARTIFICIAL INTELLIGENCE DEFINED. In this section, the term "artificial intelligence" includes the following:

(1) Any artificial system that performs tasks under varying and unpredictable circumstances without significant human oversight, or that can learn from experience and improve performance when exposed to data sets.

(2) An artificial system developed in computer software, physical hardware, or other context that solves tasks requiring human-like perception, cognition, planning, learning, communication, or physical action.

(3) An artificial system designed to think or act like a human, including cognitive architectures and neural networks.

(4) A set of techniques, including machine learning, that is designed to approximate a cognitive task.

(5) An artificial system designed to act rationally, including an intelligent software agent or embodied robot that achieves goals using perception, planning, reasoning, learning, communicating, decision making, and acting.

This is by all appearances a much meatier definition of Artificial Intelligence.

The definitional approach focuses on a concepts-oriented indication, along with a type of enumeration that depicts several variants and presumably gains added definitiveness accordingly. The preface indicates the term Artificial Intelligence *includes* those five statements, which perhaps already raises some ambiguity as to whether they are all-encompassing or merely somehow representative, and likewise whether they are each mandatory or possibly separate and independent of each other (notably, the same definition appears later on in Section 1051 of the bill, repeating the same five statements and yet prefaces it with the indication that Artificial Intelligence "includes each of the following" and thus slightly differs in the precise wording therein).

In any case, this lengthier and legally opined definition of AI is nonetheless not necessarily overly tightened or shed of any openings or loopholes. There are numerous trapdoors and pitfalls encompassed, and I'll provide a brief delectable tasting for you of especially noteworthy eye-openers.

The first statement indicates that AI is apparently a system that performs tasks "without significant human oversight" and therefore the definition appears to be striving toward the notion of incorporating autonomous operations (for more on the topic of defining AI autonomy, see my *Daily Journal* column of September 11, 2020).

On the one hand, yes, it is likely crucial to ensure that autonomy is noted as a key factor for defining AI, but in the same breath, the admission undercuts the premise by teasing with the ambiguity over the extent of human oversight. What does "without significant oversight" herald? Where does any oversight seemingly begin and end, such that we could all agree as to the degree of significant versus insignificant levels of oversight?

Envision a court case involving an alleged AI system. If the purported AI operated without human oversight for 90% of the time and required human oversight for 10% of the time, would that be sufficient to warrant being classified as an AI system under this first statement definition? What about such a system that was 99% of the time operating without human supervision and only 1% of the time with human oversight? You could readily make a compelling case that even in the lowly 1% instance, perhaps the oversight was trivial in the 99% of the time but life-determining in the 1% of the time, and thus you could argue that the tinier percentage is not a turning point per se.

Consider another quick attack at the language used.

The fifth statement indicates that AI is an "artificial system designed to act rationally," implying that being rational is the essence of AI. Why is that so? This falls into the classic trap that robots and AI are somehow going to be purely logical and rational, as though they will never be subject to presumed human frailties and foibles. I've dispelled that myth in many of my writings and analyses. In addition to that flaw in the language, it also says that the system was "designed" to such action, which leaves wide open the difference between the *design* of the AI versus the resultant *actions* of the AI.

You can drive a Mack truck through that opening.

There are numerous other issues in the stated definition of AI, glaringly too its inclusion of "machine learning" as a seemingly vital ingredient, and yet nowhere else within the body of the bill is there a definition of *Machine Learning* (yet another term bandied around these days and for which there are an exceedingly large wide variation and heated disputable meanings).

All told, at least you've now had an opportunity to take a somewhat close look at how AI has been defined, readying you for the upcoming tsunamis of AI references and inclusions into our laws, into contracts, and into the daily lives of those practicing the law.

Conclusion

A rose might be a rose by any other name, but AI is not a rose and will increasingly be used in ways that have enormous legal repercussions, as such, we ought to be prepared for speaking and writing about AI in a manner that is sensible and usable. You can bet your bottom dollar that eventually you are going to be on one side of an AI definition, perhaps arguing it to the teeth as airtight, or you'll be on the other side, clamoring that it is vacuous and inapplicable to your side of the case.

May the best argument win.

.

———————

Note: *For supplemental materials depicting the aspects discussed in this chapter, refer to Appendix B, which contains various augmented diagrams, charts, and additional related facets of relevance.*

CHAPTER 17

AI & LAW:
GROWTH IN LAWS

Key briefing points about this essay:

- A recent study estimated how many laws there are today and growth rates over time

- The research results offer vital food-for-thought about the future of the law

- Thinking outside-the-box, ponder the number of lawyers in a past, present, and future sense

- An additional twist for the future will be the advent of AI-enabled legal reasoning systems

- Advances in AI and the law might impact the number of laws and the number of lawyers

Introduction

There is a legendary adage in statistics that correlation does not denote causation.

This is an insidiously simple notion that oftentimes is entirely overlooked.

When we hear that one factor is correlated with another factor, it is easily misinterpreted to assume that there must be a cause and effect involved. A favorite such example involves a study that examined the statistical relationship between countries that tended to consume a lot of chocolate in comparison to the number of Nobel Prizes won by each respective country.

Lo and behold, there was a statistical correlation between those two factors. Does that mean that we can reasonably assume that eating more chocolate produces more Nobel Prizes? Doesn't seem to pass the smell test, despite the delicious aroma of chocolate, though one idly supposes that perhaps eating a lot of chocolate might provide some form of mental inspiration and stimulus.

In any case, shifting gears, consider the field of law. Do you know how many laws there are on the books today? How much growth has there been in the number of laws over the last twenty-five years? Is there any relationship between the number of laws and the number of lawyers? These are all intriguing and potentially important questions underlying the nature of our legal process and the national extent of our judicial efforts.

To shed some light on those questions, we'll start by taking a look at a fascinating recent study that examined the number of laws and the growth rate in the laws, doing so by using a twenty-five-year long period to try and discern any substantive patterns. After getting a sense of the landscape of the law, it might be speculative but nonetheless interesting to ponder the related matter of the number of lawyers during that same timeframe.

Beyond the topic of human lawyers, we can also consider what the future might hold if the advent of AI in the law reaches fruition and augments demonstrably the capabilities of human attorneys via the use of AI-powered autonomous legal reasoning.

The Growth In The Number Of Laws

You might know that in real estate, the infamous line is that there are three keywords to always keep in mind, namely, location, location, location. Perhaps in the field of law, one might assert that the three most notable keywords are laws, laws, laws.

Why so?

Because there is something intuitively to be said that seemingly the more laws of the land that shall exist is tantamount to stoking the number of attorneys that the world so requires. If you want to find a means to increase the number of lawyers needed in a society, presumably all you need to do is enact more laws, or so it is presumed.

Some stridently assert that there is a magical ratio for indicating how many lawyers are needed per each of the on-the-books numbers of laws that we have. If there is such a pristine quotient, this implies that by adding more laws, you will inevitably have to add more lawyers (well, unless you can make each lawyer additively productive, which we'll get to in a moment).

The reverse relationship is sometimes also claimed, such that if you were to increase the number of lawyers then the number of laws is going to be consequently increased too. The logic being that as the body of lawyers contends with a prevailing set of laws, they are undoubtedly and indubitably going to find loopholes and omissions that will get plugged up by, you guessed it, the eventual and inexorable passing of more laws. Not everyone necessarily agrees with this version of a proclaimed causation.

There is though the old joke told amongst attorneys that if there is only one lawyer in a particular town, the lawyer will starve, while if there are two attorneys in that town, they will both get rich. As a rather tongue-in-cheek saying, it does not directly argue that the number of laws will be increased when the number of lawyers increases, but some might interpret a subliminal meaning that evokes such a meaning.

Speaking of humor, it is believed that Mark Twain once stated that if you laid all the laws end to end, there would be no end to them. This is obviously a witty quip, though we know it abundantly to be untrue since there is indeed a finite number of laws that are on the books. That being said, albeit admittedly a finite number, it is nothing to sneeze at in terms of nonetheless being a whole lot of laws.

You might wonder how many laws there actually are.

Counting the number of laws is somewhat problematic. There is a nebulous sense of what constitutes a singular law per se and therefore you cannot necessarily count the number of laws as though you were counting the number of sheep or horses on a farm. The notion of crisply agreeing to what is a law and what is only a snippet of something less than law is rather ill-defined and can lead to confusion when attempting to count how many laws we have. A law might be composed of numerous legal rules, each of which stands on its own legs, and therefore you might construe those as being "laws" too.

We know at least that it is not some countless number. In other words, if we did come to a collective acknowledgment of what we mean when referring to a law, we could then proceed to count them. The effort to do the counting might be onerous and exhausting, but one way or another we could manage to count them up.

Once we counted up the number of laws, you might be wondering what would be accomplished with the count anyway?

If we have a zillion laws, does it mean that we have too many, or too few, or just the right number? Perhaps there ought to less than a zillion, one might so insist, and therefore reduce the number of laws that we are faced with. On the other hand, maybe a zillion is insufficient. It could be that we need more than a zillion, perhaps a lot more, to ensure that there aren't any ambiguities or gaps that exist due to having only a zillion laws.

It is quite a conundrum.

Recent Insightful Study On Counting Laws

A recent study by Professor Daniel Martin Katz at the Chicago Kent College of Law and serving too as a fellow colleague at the Stanford University CodeX Center for Legal Informatics of the Stanford Law School provides quite interesting insights into the counting problem and proffers a demonstrative exemplar showcasing how the counting of our laws can potentially be undertaken. In an open-access paper entitled "Complex Societies and the Growth of the Law," an effort co-authored with researchers Corinna Coupette, Janis Beckedorf, and Dirk Hartung, they crafted a computer-based model that was used to estimate the size of federal laws for the United States and also a likewise counting for Germany.

I'll focus herein on the U.S. counts.

They used twenty-five years of the US Code as found available from the Office of Law Revision Counsel of the US House Representatives and then shrewdly applied Data Science techniques to the law, covering the period from 1994 to 2018 (as an aside, I exhort that we pressingly require more Data Science savvy exertions to be applied to the field of law, which I mention to encourage up-and-coming budding lawyers and future law-oriented researchers to pursue).

We all know that laws consist of numerous sections and subsections, along with intertwining references to other associated laws, ultimately exhibiting a dense web-like network of documents and text. In brief, the computational model devised in this research study intended to examine and count the structural features of the legal corpora, focusing on counting the number of tokens (ostensibly, words of text), the number of structural elements, and the number of cross-references.

In a nutshell, the study indicates that the number of tokens in 1994 was about 14.0M and had risen to approximately 21.2M by 2018. The number of structural elements rose from 452.4K in 1994 to becoming 828.1K in 2018, and the number of cross-references went from 58.0K in 1994 to an estimated 88.6K by 2018.

All told, based on the count of tokens, there was a nearly 1.5x increase over the 25 years of 1994 to 2018. Their analysis suggests that this substantial growth in volume, connectivity, and hierarchical structure can be potentially attributed to several factors including societal expansion in the welfare arena and the area of tax.

It is an important and fascinating study.

I'd like to shift gears and carry on a bit of an outside-the-box thought experiment if you'll so indulge. Prepare yourself for an extraordinarily speculative journey (encompassing rickety assumptions underlying linearity, causation, etc.).

Lawyers And The Future

According to statistics by the American Bar Association (ABA) and the U.S. Bureau of Labor Statistics (BLS), throughout America, there were approximately 656,000 lawyers in 1994 and nearly 1,342,000 lawyers in 2018. That represents about a 2x growth in the number of lawyers during that time.

The annual increase in the number of lawyers averages 27,400 lawyers per year. The number of tokens in terms of the counting of the federal laws was rising at an average of 288,000 per year. This suggests that on a per tokens growth basis and versus the growth in the number of lawyers, there were about 10.5 tokens per attorney.

If you are willing to assume, for sake of discussion, that the growth rate in the number of tokens will continue *as is* for the next ten years, this implies that by the year 2028 (that's ten years after 2018), the number of tokens will be 24.0M. Let's also assume that the growth rate in the number of attorneys continues over that ten years and thus we would have 1.616M lawyers in 2028. This is certainly a hopeful sign for attorneys that might be worried about the prospects of jobs in the legal profession.

In any case, some believe we will witness a bountiful increase in the number of laws as a result of the advent of Artificial Intelligence (AI) as it is applied to the law. This belief is bolstered by the idea that via the use of AI, it will be easier and more friction-free for the legislative bodies to pass laws and even be aware of the potentiality of needing new laws.

Suppose we were to alter the 10-year growth rate to reflect a boost via the use of AI as applied to the law. One such modeling exercise projects that we might have 29.4M tokens by 2028, and as such, assuming the prior ratio of tokens per attorneys, we would presumably have 2.8M lawyers, an astounding 2x increase over the 2018 count.

What a glorious time to be an attorney!

Such a version of the near-term future is uplifting for those in the legal profession. Before though getting overly gleeful, one must also consider the doom-and-gloom prophecies that suggest that there will be a lessening of the number of lawyers in the coming years. A counterbalancing argument is that AI will enable lawyers to do more than they can productively do today. The advent of AI and the law will enable attorneys to work as if armed with a backhoe rather than a hand trowel.

In that case, and as alluded to earlier in this discussion, whence each attorney can do more there is seemingly no need to have as many lawyers for any given quantum of legal work, everything else being equal. In which case, just as AI is perhaps boosting the number of laws, there might be an equally countervailing use of AI by attorneys that undercuts the spurred growth in the number of attorneys. It is conceivable that the growth in the number of attorneys would be stunted, possibly even start to unravel, and perhaps the number of attorneys might stagnate all told.

The other stay-awake-at-night consideration is that the AI Legal Reasoning (AILR) computer-based prowess improves sufficiently to no longer especially need human attorneys at all.

That is the assuredly doomsday cataclysmic future for the legal profession, which, as a breather of relief, just does not seem to be in the cards within the short timeframe of ten years or so.

Conclusion

When considering what the future will hold, it seems fruitful to abide by the refrain that the future is not merely something that we fall into and instead something for which we are going to create. The manner and pace at which AI will advance and be utilized in all facets of the law are in our hands and one could assert that we are all going to invent the future thereof.

.

———

Note: *For supplemental materials depicting the aspects discussed in this chapter, refer to Appendix B, which contains various augmented diagrams, charts, and additional related facets of relevance.*

CHAPTER 18

AI & LAW:
LEGAL DESERTS

Key briefing points about this essay:

- A rising consideration in the legal profession has to do with qualms about legal deserts

- Legal deserts are geographic areas that have a dearth of available attorneys

- The public in legal deserts are potentially unable or unaware of exercising their rights

- The advent of remote access and the lure of local opportunities might aid in this matter

- In addition, the increasing use of Artificial Intelligence (AI) can play a significant role

Introduction

A desert is generally considered a rather desolate place. Trying to find food and water can be quite problematic. The chances of falling ill or expiring due to dehydration or starvation can be relatively high unless you are specially equipped for a desert trek or manage to luckily come upon an oasis.

Why all this talk about deserts and survival?

Because some liken that there are parts of the country that are essentially (so-called) *legal deserts*.

This implies that such locales are relatively barren of readily available legal advice and precludes or limits access to locally versed and available attorneys. Akin to the adverse consequences that can befall someone in an actual desert, these legal deserts portend adverse ramifications for the public at large.

Presumably, those that live in a legal desert area are likely to be underrepresented legally, oftentimes unaware of their legal rights, and unable to pursue recourse in the judicial system as a result of perchance residing in a place that has few barristers. You might suggest that there is a notable semblance of legal starvation or legal dehydration in those areas.

Some believe that these legal deserts need a hefty dose of legal advisor services and opine about ways in which this might be arranged. The most prevalent approach involves making human lawyers variously accessible, whether in-person or remotely, and meanwhile a less discussed but albeit additional possibility involves the use of Artificial Intelligence (AI) as applied to the law and legal reasoning.

Surveying The Legal Desert

Let's take a closer look at the legal desert aspects.

The ABA released its latest annual report entitled *ABA Profile of the Legal Profession 2020*, showcasing key metrics about the status of the law profession throughout the United States. This fascinating compendium provided insights into the growth of the profession and laid out a slew of visually engaging demographic analyses via a multitude of key metrics, including counts by state, by gender, by age, and so on.

New this year is a section devoted to the topic of "legal deserts," and which was noted as a relatively new term that is increasingly gaining traction in the legal field.

Per the definition proffered in the report, a legal desert is essentially a geographical area whereby residents have to travel relatively far to confer with a lawyer for needed legal advice. The advice sought might entail outstretched or extensive legal matters, or even encompass seemingly mundane or routine legal facets such as disputing a traffic ticket or drawing up a simple will.

In short, there are few if any attorneys that are physically available in these so-called legal desert locales.

This lack of within-reach legal advisors can have a variety of downsides. The public in those locales might not be aware of their legal rights and thus fail to exercise them accordingly. Furthermore, upon realizing that an attorney would be vital to their activities, the travel costs and logistic barriers to seeking and conferring with a lawyer might be prohibitive to their getting crucial legal guidance. Pundits tend to suggest that these legal deserts are further evidence supporting the contention that there is an unfortunate access-to-justice problem that sorely needs to be overcome.

Let's consider some of the eye-opening stats revealed in the report. Note that the report carefully describes the methodology used to reach the provided estimates and emphasizes that various assumptions underly the data collection and statistical analyses that were undertaken.

That being said, the first interesting stat would be that there are approximately 1.3 million lawyers in the United States.

Given that count, can you guess the top five states in terms of the states having the most lawyers?

Perhaps you have a hunch or intuition about where the predominant centers seem to be of major law offices and the like.

Here's the answer, along with the number of lawyers and their percentage of the total lawyers across the whole country:

1) New York: 184,662 lawyers (14% of the USA)

2) California: 168,569 lawyers (13% of the USA)

3) Texas: 92,833 lawyers (7% of the USA)

4) Florida: 79,328 lawyers (6% of the USA)

5) Illinois: 62,720 lawyers (5% of the USA)

If you add-up those counts and percentages, you'll see that those five states account for 588,112 of the lawyers in the U.S, amounting to 45% or nearly half of all the lawyers in America.

Of course, the use of arithmetic counting does not tell the whole story. Some states have a larger sized population and so perhaps this would tend to attract more lawyers accordingly. There might also be smaller populated states that could have as many or more lawyers per capita, despite having a lesser number of total of lawyers present in their state.

Fortunately, the report provides a per capita indication to help discern where the coverage of lawyers is either relatively high or low.

Here's then your next quick quiz.

Can you name which five states have the highest per capita of lawyers per population (based on a scale of measuring one lawyer per each one thousand residents)?

The answer is:

1) New York: 9.5 lawyers per 1,000 residents

2) Maryland: 6.7 lawyers per 1,000 residents

3) Massachusetts: 6.2 lawyers per 1,000 residents

4) Connecticut: 5.9 lawyers per 1,000 residents

5) Vermont: 5.8 lawyers per 1,000 residents

Those are the states with the highest per capita, so now see if you can guess which five states have the lowest.

Get ready, the answer is:

- Idaho: 2.2 lawyers per 1,000 residents

- South Dakota: 2.2 lawyers per 1,000 residents

- South Carolina: 2.1 lawyers per 1,000 residents

- Arkansas: 2.1 lawyers per 1,000 residents

- Arizona: 2.1 lawyers per 1,000 residents

Overall, the nationwide average is about 4 lawyers per 1,000 residents. And, as seen via the listings herein, the highest per capita is 9.5 and the lowest is 2.1.

Keep in mind that those are based on state-level populations. When you delve into the county or county-equivalent levels, the picture becomes rather bleak when it comes to the number of areas throughout the US that lack lawyers in their locale.

For about 40% of the counties and their equivalents, there is less than one lawyer per 1,000 residents, oftentimes amounting to none at all in that locale.

It is hard to definitively gauge the impacts of these legal deserts.

We can easily know the supply side by these counts but likewise knowing what the demand would be is difficult to ascertain. Even if you were to ask people whether they felt bereft of having a local lawyer, many might not realize what a lawyer could aid them in. There is also the factor of induced demand, namely that once people realize a resource is available, they tend to start making use of that resource, which otherwise the demand for the resource was unrealized.

Resourcing Legal Deserts

What might be done about these legal deserts?

An obvious approach is to somehow lure lawyers to physically reside in the locales that seem to have low per capita counts. This is not especially straightforward since there might be an insufficient need in a given locale and a lawyer so positioned might find themselves unable to make a living there.

Another approach to consider involves remote lawyering or sometimes coined as virtual law offices.

Lawyers in major cities and otherwise higher per capita locales might be able to serve those in these legal deserts via remote capabilities. The pandemic has become a kind of wake-up call about working remotely, including for those in the legal profession. If this tendency continues post-COVID, it could establish that lawyers working off-site are acceptable by the legal profession and the courts, along with getting the public used to the idea too.

You can even turn this somewhat on its head and suggest that lawyers currently residing in high per capita geographies might find it desirable to relocate to locales that have few lawyers in place today. Doing so could allow for a change in how one lives their life, possibly lowering day-to-day living costs, and keep them busy due to handling local legal needs and still providing their skills for the locale that once resided in.

Another factor is the rising capability of LegalTech and AI systems.

Lawyers using the latest in LegalTech and AI are likely to find that practicing law remotely is supported and emboldened via online applications in the cloud, allowing them to work from anywhere while remaining in touch with their colleagues, including using tools such as e-discovery, contract life cycle management, AI-powered legal chatbots, and the like. This avid use of electronic online systems readily allows for the sharing of pertinent legal info with others, regardless of whether the stakeholders are nearby or far away.

Conclusion

Legal deserts do not need to remain as they are.

Via the advent of remote working tools and advanced LegalTech applications, lawyers can reach out into those deserts to provide a lifeline. Furthermore, some lawyers might overtly choose to move into those legal deserts, serving as a local legal oasis that can help turn the sparse legal landscape into one thriving with justice.

Time to turn legal deserts into thriving lands of equal access to justice.

.

———————

Note: *For supplemental materials depicting the aspects discussed in this chapter, refer to Appendix B, which contains various augmented diagrams, charts, and additional related facets of relevance.*

CHAPTER 19

AI & LAW:

OPEN RECORDS

Key briefing points about this essay:

- There are strident calls for greater open access to court records

- Doing so will provide vital data needed for holistic policy analyses of justice

- Another important use would aid in bolstering the advent of AI in the law

- AI that utilizes Machine Learning requires extensive data to be suitably trained

- Via plentiful access to court data the efforts to devise AI Legal Reasoning would be aided

Introduction

Court records in the United States are not as readily accessible as one might assume. In a sense, there is an abundant amount of friction that prevents a full semblance of openness to court records. Various potential opportunities to better understand our system of justice and proffer modifications or enhancements are presumably being stymied.

There has been an increasing widespread call for enabling greater open access to court records of the US justice system. Despite court records generally being considered within the public domain, it is a bridge too far to presume that those archives are sufficiently available. The rub according to those making such a clamor is that there are excessive financial and technical obstacles in the way of readily being able to get access to the vast corpus (see *Science*, July 10, 2020, on "How to build a more open justice system").

Those expressing these concerns point to the onerous fact that federal court records are typically charged at about ten cents per printed page to access a case online. Though ten cents seems like a minuscule amount, if you were to multiply that dime by the likely hundreds or thousands of possible pages in a protracted case, and then multiply that by hundreds of thousands of cases nationwide, the final tab to obtain any large-scale set of court records is undoubtedly in a sky-high costly range.

Yet another significant hurdle is that court records are oftentimes in varying formats and structured unalike, meaning that even if a sizable set is purchased, trying to rationalize and align the obtained data can be burdensome and exacerbate the cost of trying to sift through them.

Critics of this status quo are apt to vehemently argue that the barriers of access to court records woefully undercuts the availability of vital data needed for holistic policy analyses of justice in America. If the bleak situation were rectified, doing so would inevitably improve the practice of law and further enhance the overall administration of justice.

Attorneys using any of the numerous commercial legal services entities that have already procured and downloaded various court records might contend that there is no need to seek out the records directly from the federal government since instead, you can get those records from those paid services. Though this path might to some degree ameliorate the formatting issues, it typically does not resolve the cost-related barriers.

There are encouraging signs of open source alternatives that tend to use crowdsourcing as a means of establishing databases of court records that are then made essentially free to access, supported at times by generous donors or sometimes via ad-based sponsors, but those datasets are not necessarily considered at a large enough scale, plus their sustainability is not relatively assured as those entities continually grapple to keep their aspirational projects afloat.

The oft-cited solution to the entire matter involves getting Congress to repeal the laws that authorize the judiciary to charge fees for access to court records.

Be forewarned, a tide of controversy muddies this straightforward proposal and centers on the root of most issues, the money involved. It turns out that those paid-for court record access fees are relatively substantial when totaled up. Estimates suggest on the order of $145 million in the fiscal year 2019 alone was derived from fees as part of the federal judiciary budget, and so the question immediately arises as to what funding would be newly surfaced to then plug the gap after making those court records available for free going forward.

Usefulness of Court Records

Shifting for the moment beyond the matter of how to assure that court records are more openly accessible, you might be wondering what would be done with those court records if they were indeed freely available.

It is assumed and hoped that a vast corpus of court records that was frictionless for access would enable researchers and scholars an increased opportunity to analyze aspects of the justice system and the nature of our courts in ways that heretofore have been prohibitively costly to undertake. In addition, journalists would potentially be bolstered in their reporting on court trends throughout the United States, and the general public would potentially become more readily engaged in what our courts are doing.

There is another beneficial possibility that does not as yet meet the eye, though gradually will have an increasing bearing on this topic, namely the advent of AI LegalTech.

Data is considered the lifeblood of AI and without it, the AI cannot function and nor flourish.

A brief explanation might help in showcasing why data is so crucial for enabling AI LegalTech.

One of the most visible and commonly applied uses of AI consists of Natural Language Processing (NLP), which we all generally experience daily via uses of Alexa, Siri, and other NLP-enabled apps. Perhaps you've recently used an e-Discovery software package that had NLP added to it or performed an online query of a contracts database using a modern NLP capability.

AI insiders know that a significant booster to NLP has been the infusion of Machine Learning (ML). Machine Learning consists of computer-based pattern matching and underlies many of the latest advances in AI. There is no magic involved, which regrettably sometimes is implied by those hyping ML, and it is wise instead to think of Machine Learning as a statistical method on steroids (kind of like multiple regression that you might have learned while in college, but more advanced). Machine Learning is a hidden element that bolsters NLP and sits inside many other AI applications too.

Leveraging Data For AI Legal Reasoning

This brings us now to the cusp of how the hindrance of access to court records relates to AI LegalTech.

When formulating an AI Machine Learning application, there is customarily a need to have data, lots of data, since you need to train the ML, of which a crucial means to do so consists of feeding in immense masses of relevant data.

Consider again the nature of multiple regression, as an illustration, showcasing that if you have too little data to feed into a regression analysis, you are sketchily on the thinnest of ground when making any bold assertions about what you have discovered. There is just not enough data there to reach valid conclusions.

If we are going to have AI LegalTech gradually become utilized as a kind of sophisticated sidearm legal advisor, the odds are that Machine Learning is going to be a crucial path to that aim, and, in turn, Machine Learning needs mega-scale sets of legal data for training purposes. Thus, besides the other overall reasons to seek a vast and freely available corpus of court records, another notable justification involves the ongoing ambitions of applying AI to the law.

Conclusion

Admittedly, there can be a dual-edged sword to this matter in that if such data is improperly used for enabling untoward AI (or, misused in other ways that have nothing to do with AI), the resultant legal rendering outputs would be dubious and suspect.

Nonetheless, it would seem ill-stated to suggest that keeping such vital data at bay is warranted, and the upside argument underlying the hoped-for benefits seems to convincingly outweigh the possibilities of any miscast incursions.

Note: *For supplemental materials depicting the aspects discussed in this chapter, refer to Appendix B, which contains various augmented diagrams, charts, and additional related facets of relevance.*

CHAPTER 20

AI & LAW:

OPENAI GPT-3

Key briefing points about this essay:

- GPT-3 is an AI-based software tool proffered by the for-profit firm OpenAI

- Acts like a souped-up "autocomplete" taking seed text and producing output text

- Was computationally trained via scrapping data across the Internet

- Legal profession applicability such as able to auto-generate contracts

- Potential legal liability issues regarding auto-generating medical advice, etc.

Introduction

There is an abundance of attention going toward a recently released software tool called GPT-3 that embraces AI techniques and, in some ways, showcases the surprisingly adept capabilities of automatically generating natural language text including producing lengthy narratives of an impressive degree.

Unfortunately, existing limitations and the questionable manner of the input data utilized to train this particular AI tool bodes for hidden dangers and indubitably reveals the severe limitations in this latest state-of-the-art technology.

For the legal profession, GPT-3 and its ilk can provide some handy assistance in the practice of law. For example, using a modicum of some initial text, you can potentially have the AI tool produce an entire contract, albeit not based on any semblance of legal logic per se and instead merely due to regurgitating text and potentially fabricating dubious new text.

Another avenue for legal interest involves the possibility that the use of GPT-3 in certain domains might raise thorny issues of liability. Consider the use case of such an AI tool for dispensing medical advice on an auto-generated basis and the specter of offering misleading or outright damaging medical guidance looms large.

Digging Into GT-3

What does GPT-3 do?

In essence, it is an autocomplete capability akin to when you compose an email or write correspondence and the computer tries to fill in what you might want to say next. We've all experienced the anticipatory facets of starting a sentence with something like "Haven't seen" and the next thing you suddenly see appear on the screen as potential next words are "you in a while." Thus, the system examined your first few words, looked-up what typically follows those words, and then presents for your ease of use the templated words that might fit your needs.

All well and good. If you don't like the words presented by the computer, you merely overwrite them with whatever you prefer to indicate instead. On the other hand, if you like the proffered words, you can readily accept them and proceed, thereby reducing the amount of effort on your part to compose your message.

The autocomplete can be a handy timesaver and reduce the amount of work required to write messages.

The twist involving GPT-3 is that it is akin to the autocomplete feature but stoked on steroids, going far beyond the everyday autocomplete that you are used to leveraging.

Let's dig into GPT-3 and examine how it has eclipsed the usual formulation of being yet another vanilla auto-complete function.

Standing for Generative Pre-Trained Transformer (GPT), this particular version is the third major instance of the capability, coined therefore as GPT-3. Released in beta use just a month ago by the company OpenAI, a for-profit AI firm located in the Bay Area of California, GPT-3 is a significant advancement over its prior siblings. One of the key differences entails the vastness of the training data used to give the autocomplete its facility to do the fill-in of anticipatory text.

The AI program is considered pre-trained, having examined millions upon millions of prior passages of online text, and can generate anticipatory text that is not just a word-for-word of what it has seen but then also transform the wording to try and better fit the circumstances involved. That's why it has been given a designated naming that includes the keywords to generate, pre-trained, and transformer.

For the training of GPT-3, the system was allowed to crawl across the enormity of the Internet, seeking out any kind of text imaginable. Besides sucking up all of Wikipedia (the English version), the algorithm scanned online digitized books, tons of articles, slews of poetry, and so on. It has been formulated upon a slurp of whatever text and at times images that it happened upon.

Where this potentially can payoff is that rather than merely providing a few words of anticipatory text, the GPT-3 can provide a boatload of text for you. If you start a sentence with "Four score and seven years ago" then the GPT-3 could respond with the rest of the entirety of the Gettysburg Address.

At first, this seems somewhat simplistic in that it would appear as though it is just grabbing up text that previously was recorded in its database. You could do a query online on your own to find the Gettysburg Address so why does it help to have a tool to do the same thing?

In theory, the GPT-3 will potentially be able to modify the anticipatory text, honing it to your particular circumstances. Now, in the case of the Gettysburg Address, it would seem unlikely that you want the words to be altered. Likely, you want to have the words as they were originally stated. This then brings up one of the possible downsides of a tool like GPT-3, namely that it might or might not retain the word-for-word version of what it earlier saw, and might too opt to provide a modified variant of what it previously had seen.

I believe it was the immortal Forest Gump that famously said that you never know what you might find in a box of chocolates.

So, the good news is that the autocomplete of GPT-3 can do some might impressive feats of writing, potentially generating an entire passage of text that was prompted by your only needing to enter a few words. The resultant passage could be unique and innovative, blending a cornucopia of many other texts that the GPT-3 algorithm has opted to intermix into the resulting output. From just a few starter words as a prompt, GPT-3 could craft an entire thousands-long worded story or narrative for you.

GPT-3 is making use of artificial neural networks, a type of software approach that tries to somewhat simulate the neural network capabilities of the brain, though in a far less capable manner and dissimilar in many material respects. In the AI field, these techniques are referred to as Machine Learning and Deep Learning. Via computationally analyzing the text that it has been fed, the GPT-3 has attempted to identify mathematical patterns and perform a richness of pattern matching across and among the plethora of text input that it has uncovered.

GPT-3 and similar auto-generating tools can be used in spurious and nefarious ways.

A simple example might suffice. Some are worried for example that students in schools will opt to use GPT-3 to write their essays for them. A sneaky student merely accesses GPT-3 (side note: it is not widely available per se while still in beta) and could generate a ten-page essay based on inputting a handful of instigating words or phrases. The output is typically being sown together via the GPT-3's Natural Language Processing (NLP) capacity, such that the text is relatively fluent looking and has the appearance of being written by a human hand.

Of course, like all of today's NLP, there are still times at which the computer-based translation is detectable, perhaps due to repeated wording or awkward or oddball phrases. Inexorably, these kinds of giveaways or gotchas are gradually being excised and the AI is being advanced to produce text that seems nearly indistinguishable from something a human might have written.

Downfalls Aplenty

A big problem with this system-generated text is that the AI of today has absolutely no semblance of reasoning, no capability of invoking common-sense, and produces text on a pretty much monkey-see-monkey-do basis. You might be aware that theorists have oft postulated that a monkey armed with a typewriter could ultimately produce the works of Shakespeare, known as the infinite monkey theorem in the computer science field, and we are seemingly getting closer to that day.

In the case of the student using GPT-3 to create an essay, the end-result might seem well crafted and inspirational, yet the AI system has not done this in any purposeful way. Instead, the GPT-3 has managed to weave together snippets of text and done so to the degree that it sure seems like it makes a lot of sense.

Well, it ought to potentially be sensible since it is based on what humans have written. If humans are writing sensible things, and if the AI is parroting those writings, the outcome should presumably be sensible too.

Unfortunately, this kind of rote mimicry also means that the untoward stuff written by humans is getting carried lock, stock, and barrel into the GPT-3 generative output too. There are already numerous instances of GPT-3 readily producing outputs that smack of racism, sexist remarks, and a plethora of other disgusting stereotypes and biases. This should not be surprising in that if you look at what is posted on the Internet, there is plenty of crazy and ill-advised text that can be absorbed by an automated crawler that just wants any text that it can find.

This old and yet trusty line still works: Garbage in, garbage out.

There is plenty of textual and narrative garbage on the Internet. Imagine all those nutty manifestos, the conspiracy theories about the world, and all of those incendiary commentaries and postings that rattle around. Much of that blithering flotsam is being potentially mixed into heralded works such as the Gettysburg Address and all other prized writings of humanity via these generative transformer tools.

Now that you've got the gist of GPT-3, keep in mind too that there are other similar generative AI-based tools in the marketplace, let's consider how these pertain to the practice of law.

Legal Profession Interest And Impacts

First, when you are next tasked with writing a new contract, using a tool such as GPT-3 could be a big booster, allowing the AI to compose a contract draft that might be quite close to what you had in mind. This is more likely if the generative tool is focused on legal contracts, rather than being trained across all kinds of texts and documents, since the language of a contract is not usually the same language used in Shakespeare or manifestos.

Second, some believe that a generative AI tool could answer questions. Right now, some have been using GPT-3 to answer medical oriented questions. You type in a health-related question, and the GPT-3 spits out text that pertains (hopefully) to the medical question you have posed. This is not hard to envision since the generative tool likely might have picked-up the same question being asked at numerous web medical sites and has been able to find consistent patterns as to the answers usually logged.

Suppose that this same capacity was used to try and answer legal questions. Yes, it could certainly be attempted. Of course, similar to qualms about answering medical questions, one has to recoil somewhat at the veracity of whatever answers might be given via a tool such as GPT-3. There is also the open question as to whether this kind of AI tool is going over-the-line, as it were, and entering into the act of practicing the law, something that remains an ongoing debate inside and outside of the law profession.

Another legal facet involves the potential for legal liability associated with a generative AI tool like this. Suppose a company sets up a generative piece of software and offers it to the public as a means of answering questions about medical matters. What kind of liability might this create for the company taking such actions? Despite any potential disclaimers, there might nonetheless still be liabilities to be incurred.

A recurring issue with much of the AI that is being fostered into the marketplace has to do with the inscrutability of the systems. An AI package being used to decide who gets a car loan or a home loan might be using hidden biases based on training data that contains those biases, but no one necessarily realizes those biases existed. Efforts to try and get AI to be explainable, known as XAI or explainable-AI, are being pushed by those in the AI Ethics realm.

A generative tool like GPT-3 has already received criticism for its lack of XAI, meaning that when it produces its output, there are no direct means to trace where it came from and how it was derived.

Meanwhile, the output can readily be jammed with misinformation. The convincing nature of how well it seems written will cloak the underlying biases and falsehoods.

If you were already worried about the Internet and its writings, generative tools are going to up the ante and be able to produce even more gobs of narratives to be found online and infused into social media and tweets. An autocomplete capability has a lot of potential handiness and likewise can be a bear to deal with. You can simply turn off the feature when composing an email or a document but doing likewise for the Internet is not feasible and we might end-up with incredibly "new" writings of soaring maxims while getting overfilled with outrageous rants and untoward raves.

Conclusion

AI-enabled tools such as GPT-3 are going to continue to be fostered and incrementally improved.

Meanwhile, the application of these auto-generative text capabilities will increasingly be applied to the field of law, showing up as standalone LegalTech or immersed into existing LegalTech.

In addition, you can expect that when these auto-generative machinations are used in various domains, inevitably there will be legal questions raised about what AI is doing, how the AI came to be and will spur the judicial system to step into the matter and aid in resolving a likely cacophony of disputes and difficulties that will inexorably appear.

Note: *For supplemental materials depicting the aspects discussed in this chapter, refer to Appendix B, which contains various augmented diagrams, charts, and additional related facets of relevance.*

CHAPTER 21
AI & LAW:
LEGAL JUDGMENT PREDICTION

Key briefing points about this essay:

- Lawyers are continually having to try and predict what will happen in a legal case

- Legal Judgment Prediction (LJP) involves devising computer models for making such predictions

- The use of Artificial Intelligence (AI) is aiming to boost the predictive capabilities of LJP

- There are advantages and also downsides to using AI-powered LJP predictions

- If AI LJP becomes superbly predictive it could have a dramatic judicial impact

Introduction

You might say that lawyers are inexorably in the continual midst of making predictions. They do so while in the middle of a legal battle, they do so once a case result is proclaimed and thus have to predict whether an appeal might follow, they make predictions before a case even gets underway, and so on.

Being in the legal field is a boatload of predicting, along with facing numerous underwater minefields and other hidden dangers when trying to make such predictions.

For example, when considering whether to take a new case, an astute attorney will ruminate on the nature of the legal issues involved and what the likely outcome of the case might be. A client seeking legal counsel will undoubtedly expect their potential legal advisor to offer some indication of how the case is going to turn out.

Typically, prudent lawyers are hesitant to make outright unequivocal predictions per se and instead proffer what they likely believe or generally anticipate the outcome will be, casting the prediction as shrouded in potential complications. Thus, somewhat safely distancing themselves from a seemingly ironclad prediction, emphasizing the inexorable uncertainties involved in making prophecies about any guarantee of legal results.

Newbie attorneys sometimes get themselves into quite hot water by making bold proclamations as though they possess an unerring legal-beagle crystal ball. Besides inevitably opening themselves to potential accusations or pursuit of legal malpractice, they are undoubtedly going to find themselves on the wrong side of a soured client that later on recalls how assuredly boastful the initial prediction was, particularly if the case goes astray of the anticipated outcome. Furthermore, a legal prediction without any semblance of qualification or leeway is at the margins of the expected ethical requirements for practicing law since it can unduly mislead a client.

In short, lawyers make predictions, but it is a touchy subject, fraught with difficulties and dangers, and entails reading tea leaves that might be messy and occluded, yet somehow has to be undertaken, preferably safely so.

Some attorneys feel like they never signed-up to be soothsayers and wonder how they got plopped into the business of being legal prediction seers.

It is rare that law schools focus much on predictions and predictive methods and therefore an attorney must via seat-of-the-pants craft and refine their own abilities to render legal predictions. It is one thing to read the daily news and pontificate idly about how the Supreme Court might rule, and something altogether more somber and serious when having to assess a case that you are personally taking on and having to predict the outcome, which will have direct consequences on you, your practice, your client, and the like.

Legal Judgment Prediction Is Afoot

Increasingly there have been efforts to utilize computer-based models to aid in making legal predictions. This field of study and application is often referred to as Legal Judgment Prediction (LJP).

The idea is to try and formalize the predictive process and supplement human conjecture with mathematical and analytic tools. Early versions of LJP consisted of spreadsheet models that were crude and simplistic. Gradually, advanced statistical models have been employed.

The advent of Artificial Intelligence (AI) as blended into the practice of law is further bolstering the predictive capabilities for attorneys. By using AI techniques such as Natural Language Processing and Machine Learning, it is becoming increasingly feasible to computationally assess a large corpus of legal cases and based upon detected patterns then make predictions for a newly presented legal case.

That being said, do not be misled into believing that today's AI for Legal Judgment Prediction is somehow sentient or superhuman in being able to render case outcome predictions. That's just not the case. In my latest research on the use of AI for Legal Judgment Prediction, I point out that we are merely still in what I refer to as the Level 2 stage, and have quite a distance to go before we can get to the autonomous futuristic kinds of AI capabilities that will arise once we enter into say Level 4 or Level 5.

Digging Deeper Into LJP

One subtle but important facet about Legal Judgment Prediction is the meaning of the word "judgment" within the moniker itself. Does the usage of the overloaded word "judgment" imply solely an outcome-oriented focus, such that it is akin to saying *Legal Outcome Prediction*, or does it mean any kind of judicial decision-making or potentiality?

Here's why this semantic parsing is crucial, perhaps painstakingly so.

Legal prediction models and allied efforts tend to exclusively aim at the outcome or final judgment of legal cases. Though this certainly is warranted and inarguably bona fide as a focal point, I've pointed out that a legal case can fruitfully employ predictive powers throughout its entire lifecycle. What might happen, for example, upon initially entering a plea for a legal case? As another example, what is going to occur midway in a legal case as to how the next step of the case is going to come out?

There are many legal battles and skirmishes on the way towards a final ending of a legal war, as it were. Yes, you want to know whether the war is going to be won or lost, and also, for those amid battle, it certainly can be insightful and instrumental to gauge whether each battle or skirmish is going to end up favorably or not.

As such, AI capabilities for Legal Judgment Prediction ought to incorporate stepwise elements into their predictive capacities. When immersed in a legal case, and at some specified stage in the lifecycle of the case, it would be immensely helpful to leverage an AI prediction LJP that could aid in assessing how the next nearest step is going to fare. Or indicate how two steps from now, or eight steps from now, what the success proclivity looks like. These indications could arm attorneys with useful insights along the arduous journey of trying a case, rather than only offering a one-time end-state indication.

This brings up another existing qualm about some aspects of Legal Judgment Prediction.

Even if we assume that LJP is referring to essentially legal *outcome* prediction, a begging question that can readily be asked is what the outcome consists of. A prediction that you will prevail in the outcome of a particularly thorny case could be completely upended by subsequent appeals. An attorney using an AI-enabled prediction system needs to know whether the "outcome" being forecasted is with respect to the (shall we say) ultimate outcome or perhaps some intermediary result that is going to ultimately be overturned.

Another concern is that the emerging AI systems for legal predictive purposes can oftentimes be inscrutable. The arcane mathematics embodied in a large-scale Artificial Neural Network, referred to as Deep Learning will rarely have any ready-made logical explanation to it. You might be delighted that the AI has predicted a favorable outcome for your case, but it does so without any kind of overt common-sense reasoning or ability to articulate how such a conclusion was derived. Whether you are willing to rely upon or trust something solely of enigmatic automation can be dicey and disquieting.

Finally, there is an enduring philosophical debate in the field of law about the intrinsic nature of the law and the role of prophecies and predictions. You might recall the famous words of renowned jurist Oliver Wendell Holmes, namely: "The prophecies of what the courts will do in fact, and nothing more pretentious, are what I mean by law." One interpretation of this now-classic statement is that perhaps the mainstay of what lawyers do is prediction, more so than merely as an afterthought or add-on to the task of practicing law.

There is also the street version of legal predictive mechanizations. Some say that you can anticipate a ruling by a judge due to how they have previously made their rulings and by inspection of their long-running historical record of jurisprudence. That's the scientific and abundantly rationalized version of LJP. Others suggest, perhaps partially in jest and partially in all seriousness, whatever the judge perchance had for breakfast on the morning of a ruling is more aptly to indicate how the judge will rule on a case in-hand (colloquially known as "digestive jurisprudence").

Conclusion

No matter how one might view the law, it seems nearly inarguable that making predictions and seeking to make on-target predictions is inescapably part of being in the field of law. That is a fundamental truth and for which improving our abilities to make legal predictions, by means such as leveraging AI, can aid in performing needed legal efforts with greater aplomb.

I'm predicting an expanding future for using AI-based prediction in the field of AI & Law and you can assuredly hold me to that prophecy.

———

Note: *For supplemental materials depicting the aspects discussed in this chapter, refer to Appendix B, which contains various augmented diagrams, charts, and additional related facets of relevance.*

CHAPTER 22

AI & LAW:

LEGAL DOCTRINES

Key briefing points about this article:

- The law consists of numerous and vital doctrines that are invented rules-of-law

- One well-known instance was first derived via a court case of the wagon and the donkey

- AI is anticipated to gradually and inexorably become adept at AI-based legal reasoning

- An unresolved question entails how such AI systems will be imbued with law doctrines

- By exploring the doctrine rising the wagon and donkey we can gauge Machine Learning (ML)

Introduction

There is a quite legendary court case that entails a wagon and a donkey, dating back to 1842 and become a foundation for a legal doctrine that was eventually transferred from English law into American law. This law-expanding case involved a horse-drawn wagon that rammed into and sadly overran a donkey.

Can you name the case?

Can you also name the area of law that was forever changed due to the case?

Take a moment and search your mental legal corpus to try and ferret out what the answer is. A bit of a puzzler, perhaps, so let's proceed into the details of the case and then provide a grand reveal, though you might otherwise have sooner guessed the crux of the matter once you have been given a deeper set of clues.

Here's the saga.

A stagecoach style wagon was being driven by a man that was employed by a wagon owner. The wagon was rumbling along on a dirt road that was relatively well-marked and had delineated boundaries marking either side of the roadway. The driver was seated in the wagon and sat behind a team of three horses that were pulling the wagon.

So far, those facts seem to be clear cut and lacking in dispute, thus take them as a given.

A donkey had been tethered to a post that was nearby the road. The man that owned and tethered the donkey stepped away and was not immediately present to continually watch over the donkey. Since a donkey is a donkey, and they oft wander to-and-fro, the donkey opted to meander as far as it might, subject to the limits of the tethered rope.

Those facts also seem to be without any discord in this legal case.

Unfortunately, things take a turn for the worse.

The donkey ends up standing in the roadway, still tethered, but having wandered nonetheless into an active thoroughfare. The wagon comes along. Alas, the driver apparently does not see the donkey and therefore does not take any action to try and stop the wagon, nor steer away from the donkey.

The team of charging horses' rams into the donkey, knocking the animal to the ground. The donkey gets trampled and dies soon thereafter.

The owner of the donkey, the plaintiff in the subsequent legal case, sues the owner of the wagon, the defendant, and contends that the wagon was being operated inappropriately and that the actions of the owner/operator-led indisputably to the death of his donkey.

Okay, you've now been provided with the foundational facts, though I am admittedly somewhat cheekily holding out a few finer details and those will certainly tip you to the root of the matter.

Here is a recap of the declaration as filed for the case:

"The declaration stated, that the plaintiff theretofore, and at the time of the committing of the grievance thereinafter mentioned, to wit, was lawfully possessed of a certain donkey, which said donkey of the plaintiff was then lawfully in a certain highway, and the defendant was then possessed of a certain wagon and certain horses drawing the same, which said wagon and horses of the defendant were then under the care, government, and direction of a certain then servant of the defendant, in and along the said highway; nevertheless the defendant, by his said servant, so carelessly, negligently, unskillfully, and improperly governed and directed his said wagon and horses, that by and through the carelessness, negligence, unskillfulness, and improper conduct of the defendant, by his said servant, the said wagon and horses of the defendant then ran and struck with great violence against the said donkey of the plaintiff, and thereby then wounded, crushed, and killed the same."

Even just a quick glance at this legal predicament suggests that this case revolves around a question of negligence, which is ostensibly abundantly obvious as we have someone that presumably has been negligent in their actions and ergo led to the death of the donkey.

You might be eyeing the defendant as being negligent because, well, the operator of the wagon undeniably ran over and killed the donkey. On the other hand, you might be looking sternly at the plaintiff, since he tethered his donkey in a locale that was fraught with danger and did not seem to exercise due care for his beast of burden.

Another viewpoint is that perhaps they are both equally at fault, is a type of regrettable status quo condition, whereby the donkey owner should not have tethered the donkey such that it could wander onto the path of the wagon or that he should have stood to watch and been there to prevent his donkey from getting into an ill-advised quandary. In that light, you might also find equal fault with the wagon driver for not having stopped or averted hitting the donkey, and thus cancel out the two separate but intertwined wrongs as though they were unlucky counterbalancing forces of nature.

Time To Reveal The Case

You have assuredly summarized that this case has to do with tort law and the role of comparative negligence versus contributory negligence.

In particular, what new doctrine was borne out of this case?

If you are wavering back-and-forth about the potential actions of the wagon driver and the actions of the owner of the donkey, here's an added facet of the case that might sway you and be construed as a pivotal element. I'll also name the case, it was *Davies v. Mann* (152 Eng Rep 588, 1842).

During the trial, it was indicated by a witness that the wagon was coming along at a "smartish pace" and this seemed to measure heavily in the minds of the court, and eventually likewise pivotal for the appellate court that heard the case after it was appealed.

At trial, the defendant was found to be negligent, based on the logic that if there had been a semblance of ordinary or reasonable care exercised then the donkey would not have been killed (i.e., the alleged smartish pace was akin to an overburdening leaden weight pushing voraciously down upon the scales of justice).

It was theorized that the wagon driver had a *last clear chance* to avoid the ramming of the donkey yet had failed to undertake that chance. Of course, today we know this as the famous "last clear chance" doctrine, sometimes also referred to as the last opportunity rule.

For some final details about the famous or perhaps infamous case of the wagon and the donkey, there was upon appeal the question raised as to whether the donkey was illegally in the roadway and thus this made the stance for the defendant even stronger and surely weakened the position of the plaintiff. But, surprisingly (or scandalously), this assertion had not been apparently raised as a notable point of contention at trial by the defense.

The appellate ruling proffered that whether the donkey might or might not have been legally or illegally placed was essentially immaterial, and concluded therein: "All that is perfectly correct; for, although the [donkey] may have been wrongfully there, still the defendant was bound to go along the road at such a pace as would be likely to prevent mischief. Were this not so, a man might justify the driving over goods left on a public highway, or even over a man lying asleep there, or the purposely running against a carriage going on the wrong side of the road."

The notion of the last clear chance doctrine came squarely into U.S. law during a case in North Carolina of *Gunter v. Wicker* (85 N.C. 310, 1881). Was it another instance of a wagon and a donkey? Nope.

This case in 1881 involved a man that was working in a sawmill and had been employed to do several tasks including the oiling of the equipment.

At one point, a saw was purposely stopped to allow for the oiling activity, the man entered into the flywheel to provide an oil coating and horrifically was injured when the owner/operator at the sawmill turned on the steam and for which caused serious injuries to the oiler.

At trial, the oiler as the plaintiff contended that the sawmill owner/operator was negligent in having turned on the steam while the oiler was inside the machinery. The owner/operator as the defendant argued that the oiler had put himself into danger by maneuvering into the flywheel and that such posturing was unnecessary to do the oiling task.

The ruling made was that despite acknowledging that the oiler had put himself into harm's way, possibly even needlessly so, nonetheless the steam would only become injurious due to the actions of the defendant by having turned on the steam at the wrong time.

In short, the key takeaway was that the sawmill owner/operator had the *last clear chance* to avoid the injurious incident but failed to exercise ordinary or reasonable care in doing so. A probing legal analysis of the last clear chance doctrine was conducted in 1926 by Matthew Myers and published in the *North Carolina Law Review* (see volume 5, number 1). Though the doctrine was still relatively nascent at the time, it had already been used in a multitude of court cases regarding railroad accidents. According to Myers: "The North Carolina Court holds a defendant liable not only where he has the last clear chance and knows of it, but where he has the last clear chance and doesn't know of it, but would have known of it if he had not been negligent."

Today's modern world certainly has plentiful examples of legal cases that dovetail into the last clear chance doctrine. Rather than a wagon and a donkey, envision a driver of a car that strikes a pedestrian crossing the street. If that isn't modern enough for you, consider the instance of a so-called self-driving car that struck and killed a pedestrian in Phoenix, Arizona just a few years ago, and ask yourself whether the last clear chance doctrine will come to play in a world filled with AI-based autonomous vehicles.

AI In The Law And The Role Of Doctrines

Speaking of AI, let's take a moment and reconsider the last clear chance doctrine in a completely different light.

In Chapter 2, I posited that we will eventually see that AI will become infused into the law via advancements in autonomous levels of legal reasoning. AI systems will be able to aid lawyers and attorneys via serving as an over-the-shoulder legal oriented advisory tool.

Inevitably, this capability will be further improved such that the question will arise as to whether the AI-powered legal reasoning can effectively practice law, as it were, doing so without any human lawyer being involved. This is an open-ended matter and we have yet to witness AI of that caliber, though this does not necessarily imply that we aren't headed down that path.

Ponder the next question as it will be the basis for a macroscopic perspective on how AI will become ingrained in the law and possibly become an active legal reasoner.

How would an AI system become versed in the *last clear chance* doctrine?

Seems like a relatively straightforward question. There is no denying that we would expect any fully enabled AI legal reasoning system to be able to grasp the nature of the last clear chance doctrine. It is assuredly a topic covered for budding human lawyers and typically tested as part of any bar exam. Any attorney worth their salt should have some familiarity with the doctrine, regardless of whether it is avidly utilized in their chosen specialty of law.

Some might suggest that the AI could use Machine Learning (ML) as a means of coming up-to-speed about this particular doctrine. For clarification, today's notion of Machine Learning is really a mathematical approach that uses computational pattern matching to try and find discernible patterns in data. Think of a statistical tool such as multiple regression and that's generally the same idea.

I point this out because some have ascribed mystical qualities to Machine Learning, as though it is akin to the way that humans learn, but this is a misleading and astronomically overstated exaggeration of what this type of Machine Learning can do.

Okay, so we need lots of data to feed into the pattern matching, and out of which will hopefully arise identified patterns.

Without going into a mode of reductio ad absurdum, pretend that we were able to collect hundreds or possibly thousands of legal cases encompassing a wagon and a donkey. The data consisted of the raw facts of the case and the resulting decision. Assume that the last clear chance doctrine is not specifically called out. Your only recourse to discerning the doctrine would be by the implied pattern of the facts of the case and the outcomes of the cases.

Does it seem reasonable to expect that the pattern matching would eventually land onto a doctrine, devised by its own pattern detection, which otherwise resembled the last clear chance rule?

That's a hard one to answer with any certainty.

It is possible that the raw data could be analyzed mathematically to the degree that a mathematical result would approximate the last clear chance doctrine. On the other hand, there might other patterns discerned, some that might be contrary to the last clear chance or be somewhat byzantine and defy any everyday logical explanation.

Think of this as though a computer has analyzed zillions of chess games and found computationally complex patterns that might not readily be translatable into an overarching strategy of how to play chess. Thus, you end-up with an inscrutably good, automated chess player that frustratingly, for us humans, cannot explain why this is so.

This then brings us to the crux of why I've brought up the entire discussion about the last clear chance doctrine. It wasn't conveyed as simply an engaging rehash underlying the history of the doctrine, nor was it intended as any kind of revelation about this now-classic longstanding legal rule. The point here is more so about how we are going to approach the application of AI into the law, along with the nature of how this anticipated AI will be suitably able to inject legal reasoning and the law.

Machine Learning As A Doctrine Seer

One approach being heralded are the latest techniques underlying Machine Learning.

Though this bodes for an exciting promise, there are inherent limitations, some say dangers, whereby the AI so crafted would not find the patterns that we humans have already invented, such as the last clear chance doctrine. Furthermore, the AI might seemingly detect such patterns and then use those to act upon the law, performing the services of an attorney or a judge, and yet we might not have any viable means of logically ascertaining how the AI is performing those legal tasks.

The AI could conceivably come up with a *combobulation doctrine*, something that either is an oddball rule that defies rational explanation or might ironically reveal a new and ostensibly useful doctrine that humans had not heretofore devised.

There is an ongoing debate among legal scholars and legal engineers about using an explicit approach toward arming AI with the law and legal reasoning versus doing so via an implicit avenue. In the explicit technique, you expressly program the AI with the legal rules, and those are considered ingrained or the DNA as it will of the AI system (be cautious though in overstepping such an analogy, we ought to avoid anthropomorphizing the AI).

Others contend that this is a grueling path, taking too much time, and would involve a lowest-common-denominator level of granularity that we might find intractable and impossible to ultimately attain for any proficiency across-the-board about the law. Thus, they would propose the Machine Learning angle be leveraged instead, allowing the AI to somewhat train itself, as it were, rather than being fed inches at a time by a human hand.

Some refer to this in the AI field all told as the ongoing and acrimonious debate or battle between the symbolics and the sub-symbolics.

The symbolics consists of those that tend toward being explicit and programming the AI to do its desired tasks (recall the earlier days of AI and the use of expert systems and knowledge-based systems), while the sub-symbolics insist that the AI has to train itself (via the use of Artificial Neural Networks and the likes of Machine Learning and Deep Learning). Per any field or specialty, some sit at the extremes of those two poles, while some prefer to try and blend the two positions.

Conclusion

In the future, I suppose that if any of us ever perchance leave our donkey tied-up nearby to a road, and a wagon comes along, we would hope that the AI adjudication system would be versed in the last clear chance doctrine. Since that is a futuristic scenario, substitute a self-driving car for the wagon, but I guess we can retain the donkey in that setting since we are going to hopefully still have donkeys, as cantankerous as they might be.

Of course, per the legendary proverb, one should never stand before a judge and nor behind a donkey.

Note: *For supplemental materials depicting the aspects discussed in this chapter, refer to Appendix B, which contains various augmented diagrams, charts, and additional related facets of relevance.*

CHAPTER 23

AI & LAW:
TECH-HYPE CURVES

Key briefing points about this essay:

- Tech-Hype curves showcase which tech is being over-hyped and which tech is settling in

- Each year the Gartner Group releases iterations of their famous Tech-Hype curves

- Recent AI & Law advances were categorized by Gartner's latest LegalTech hype curve

- Upcoming are legal chatbots, third-party risk management, AI in legal practices, etc.

- But some AI & Law tech efforts are predicted as doomed, others are on verge of a reboot

Introduction

To get any media attention these days, it seems that sometimes being egregiously overboard and making nearly laughably exaggerated claims is the only way to rise above the fray. This especially happens in the tech field and particularly in the realm of Artificial Intelligence (AI).

Ostensibly, each new AI system is proclaimed as the absolute incarnation of human cognition and heralded as the final arrival of computer-based sentience. Though at first glance this might seem innocent and able to be simply shrugged off as obvious hyperbole, the reality is that distorting reality is not a laughing matter and continues to promulgate falsehoods about what is capable in AI and what is still science fiction.

The realm of AI & Law is equally vulnerable to these same hyperbolic woes.

Advances in legal technology are oftentimes accompanied by a dollop of hype and bombastic overstatements. Headlines will from time-to-time tout that some new LegalTech offering is going to revolutionize the legal industry, and, via the added whiff of including AI, suggest that lawyers are going to be out of work due to a robotic legal reasoner that can do what human barristers are being paid to do.

This tomfoolery is so frequent that there are so-called tech-hype curves that have been devised and promulgated to help in separating the wheat from the chaff. One such curve by the analyst group Gartner recently was released and starkly indicated which segments of LegalTech they believe to be headed upward and which are heading downward. Having been updated for 2020, the curve includes such notable segments as legal chatbots, advanced contract analytics, e-discovery, Natural Language Processing (NLP), and the like.

I'll momentarily walk you through the indication about the segments and their status, and provide some brief commentary.

First, let's consider some overarching insights.

The segmentations and their positionings on these tech-hype curves need to be taken with a grain of salt. It is easy to slap an entire segment into the up or down categories, yet meanwhile, there can be some individual players within the segment that are either especially promising or that have regrettably entirely struck out.

Thus, do not let a broad paintbrush unduly blot or mar specific LegalTech and AI products and offerings.

There is also the matter of inadvertently assuming that those analysts devising the curves are all-knowing and are infallible in terms of how they rate or assess a given segment. LegalTech soothsayers have been wrong, many a time, and misjudged based on personal biases and preferences.

Do not necessarily worship any such curve as a final soothsayer.

Finally, consider the entire exercise as more of a means to try and grasp generally what seems to be taking hold, along with catching your breath when seeing that a favored LegalTech segment is in the doghouse. Perhaps there are facets about the segment that you are not noticing and that are aiming toward an eventual collapse.

In short, the LegalTech tech-hype curves are a handy wake-up call to keep us all from falling for too much of the shine and sparkle that accompanies those publicity-seeking LegalTech and AI purveyors.

With that discerning preamble, let's consider the nature of this particular tech-hype curve on LegalTech.

Divided into stages, the curve starts in an upward trend known as "on the rise" and ultimately reaches a peek at what is considered the topmost set of inflated expectations, after which the curve then falls into the dreaded and euphemistically coined "trough of disillusionment." If a technology segment is lucky, it will climb out of the trough and enter into a slope of enlightenment, meaning that the hype has subsided and the tech is being put to everyday use, even though it might not be able to leap tall buildings and go faster than a speeding bullet.

Eventually, a LegalTech that has made it into the slope of enlightenment will likely reach a plateau. This can be okay in that the tech might have become part-and-parcel of legal practices and thus no longer is a standout per se yet continues to provide substantive value.

These are the proposed stages and their intended trending slopes:

- Stage 1: On the rise (going up)

- Stage 2: Peak of inflated expectations (at the top and on the verge of heading down)

- Stage 3: Trough of disillusionment (sliding down into the abyss)

- Stage 4: Slope of enlightenment (climbing out of the ditch)

Here are then are various existing LegalTech segments as analyst-ordained to fall within each of those aforementioned stages:

Stage 1: On the Rise

Includes: Subject rights requests, Legal chatbots, Third-party risk management, AI in corporate legal practice, AI governance, Blockchain for data security

Here are a few quick insights about some of the more notable segments that are labeled as on the rise:

- **Legal Chatbots.** Legal chatbots are virtual agents that enter into a dialogue using Natural Language Processing (NLP) and try to offer suggestions or guidance when performing a legal related task. Such chatbots can be aimed at lawyers and legal professionals and might also be targeted at non-lawyer end-users seeking legal advice or insights. When these legal chatbots first appeared a few years ago, there was some handwringing that these AI-based agents might end-up replacing lawyers, which has decidedly not been the case and the actual capabilities have been relatively simplistic and routine. Though legal chatbots have been placed into the on the rise stage, already there is a widespread realization of their limitations and perhaps ought to be placed already into the peak of inflated expectations.

- **AI Governance.** As AI apps continue to flood the marketplace, they are at times violating various AI ethics guidelines and threatening our privacy, security, and other key socio-legal principles. Countries around the globe have come out with formalized AI Ethics stipulations, though few have been codified into law. Trying to legally regulate AI will be heralded at first, but trying to pin down a balanced approach that doesn't quash AI innovations is bound to get mired in acrimonious debate, thus this segment is regrettably likely to soon peak in terms of initial enthusiasm and get jammed-up on the shores of inflated expectations.

Stage 2: Peak of inflated expectations

Includes: Legal spend management, Data breach response, Consent, and preference management, Smart contracts, Digital ethics, Explainable AI, Alternative legal service providers, Legal and compliance analytics, Advanced contract analytics, Prescriptive analytics, Privacy impact assessments

Here are a few quick insights about some of the more notable segments that are labeled as being at the peak of inflated expectations:

- **Legal Spend Management.** Many law practices were initially hopeful that the adoption of legal spend management software would enable their offices to be better tuned to where their costs were and ultimately lead to a significant reduction in unnecessary spending. Unfortunately, in a launch-and-forget mode, some law firms set up such systems blindly, without reimagining how they run their legal services efforts. The use of these kinds of cost-cutting applications must be done judiciously, involving informed leaders and partners that don't merely impose automated spending handcuffs. These systems are not a mindless silver bullet and require concerted attention to get properly established.

- **Explainable AI.** With AI being embedded into numerous LegalTech applications, a significant concern that arose involved the inscrutable nature of what the AI was doing under-the-hood. For example, an AI LegalTech app that predicts whether you will likely prevail in your court case is bound to have all kinds of underlying assumptions based solely on precedents, and fail to consider factors that might be beyond the prior corpus of cases. Indeed, there might even be key cases that were not included in the legal database being used to train the AI. It was hoped that by including an explainability component into these AI packages it would resolve these qualms, but the result so far has been that Explainable AI (abbreviated as XAI) has yet to live up to its potential. It is going to be a while before this tech constrained situation dramatically improves.

Stage 3: Trough of disillusionment

Includes: Integrated risk management, Natural language query, Data and analytics governance, Digital business transformation, Blockchain, Robotic Process Automation (RPA), Privacy management tools

Here are a few quick insights about some of the more notable segments that are labeled as being in the dreaded trough of disillusionment:

- **Natural Language Query.** Natural Language Query is more popularly known as Natural Language Processing (NLP), of which there was an earlier hope that law professionals could directly interact with or query legal systems via using a conversational mode akin to talking with a human that is versed in the legal domain. Unfortunately, most of the NLP to-date is not versed in the legal realm per se, and oftentimes is nothing more than a knock-off of a generic kind of Alexa or Siri overlay that tries to proffer some semblance of dialoguing, but has no legal awareness chops. The good news is that gradually these NLP are getting better, along with being trained for the specifics of the legal field.

- **Blockchain.** By now, we all certainly know that blockchain mania has relatively subsided, though its cryptocurrency use still commands headlines when an occasional flare-up of various electronic coinages occurs. For the legal domain, blockchain was supposed to provide a slew of possibilities, including the ability to readily keep track of court filings, enable the creation of smart contracts, track IP rights, streamline document notarizations, and so on. Sadly, few of these have taken hold as yet. Fortunately, blockchain still fundamentally offers those capabilities and we will gradually witness blockchain-enabled systems that tackle longstanding weaknesses in existing paper-rooted practices.

Stage 4: Slope of enlightenment

Includes: Corporate legal matter management, e-Discovery software, Contract life cycle management, Enterprise legal management, Predictive Analytics, Text Analytics, Ethics, and compliance management

Here are a few quick insights about some of the more notable segments that are labeled as being in the revered slope of enlightenment:

- **e-Discovery Software.** Enlightened attorneys would likely applaud the advent of e-Discovery software, providing an at-the-fingertips electronic means of undertaking discovery and averting the traditional painstaking paper-based hunt for those crucial needles in a haystack to try and win a case. You might remember that earlier it was touted that e-Discovery would do the work for you, and this led to the segment at one point getting tossed into the trough of disillusionment since it was an outstretched expectation. Today, now that there is a pervasive balanced perspective about what e-Discovery can do, it is heading up the slope of enlightenment.

- **Contract Life Cycle Management**. Contract life cycle systems initially were overly glorified, rose to the peak of inflated expectations, dropped into the trough, and are now climbing their way out of the abyss. When appropriately put in place, these are perfunctory but also essential to well-managing any legal practice. No more losing sight of what happened to a contract being drafted, and also a handy means to make sure that contracts are timely derived and delivered.

So, how you do feel about the segment category assignments.

Do they surprise you, does it seem ho-hum, or do they perhaps irk you?

You might be pleased to see some segments in stages that you wholeheartedly agree as to where they belong, and at the same time be disgruntled to observe some other segments in stages that it seems unfair or outright inappropriate to place them.

That's the typical reaction to these tech-hype curves by anyone that already is familiar with the legal tech realm. I long ago decided to not let my blood boil on such matters and take the whole ritual in stride. Please know, if the placement of certain segments has gotten under your skin, do not let it ruin your day.

Conclusion

Of course, there is an unfortunate danger that those uninformed might bet the farm on these curves, doing so without realizing the questionable nature involved, and find themselves either missing out on great opportunities or getting sunk in an ill-advised LegalTech investment.

Bottom-line is to keep informed and get sufficiently up-to-speed to know which twist and which turn will most likely impact your favored LegalTech and AI segment.

That's the right curve to be on.

.

———

Note: *For supplemental materials depicting the aspects discussed in this chapter, refer to Appendix B, which contains various augmented diagrams, charts, and additional related facets of relevance.*

CHAPTER 24

AI & LAW:

LEGALTECH STARTUPS

Key briefing points about this essay:

- Many attorneys harbor a dream to do a startup business based on a LegalTech idea they have

- An entrepreneurial-minded lawyer needs to think ahead and prepare for the rough journey

- The good news is that the VC/PE funding for LegalTech startups still seems to be doing well

- The "bad news" is that there are lots of LegalTech flops and failures, so be forewarned

- Abide by the included list of 20 key factors for your startup and you'll have a better chance

Introduction

Many lawyers harken to startup their own business that would bring the next legal-world shattering latest-and-greatest LegalTech product to the marketplace.

Many software developers have a likewise ambition.

Oftentimes, those entrepreneurial lawyers seeking such a quest are not especially tech-savvy, but they do know the legal arena and believe they also know what attorneys need or want. As such, they hope to leverage or exploit their legal domain knowledge by getting underway with a new startup to craft the LegalTech software they envision, though whether the law-oriented application is viable to be created and technically feasible is an open question.

Meanwhile, those software developers that dream of doing a startup that showcases some exciting new technology as embedded into a LegalTech context are frequently bereft of any in-depth understanding of the practice of law. As such, they hope to leverage or exploit their software expertise and technology know-how by starting a new company that would create and brings to the market a LegalTech tech-amplified product, though whether it provides a sensible and profitable market-fit solution is an open question.

Whichever manner that you are opting to come into the LegalTech niche, there are some key precepts that you ought to be considering.

In this first of a series of articles, we'll take the perspective of the attorney that wants to move ahead with a LegalTech-related startup.

And, include a handy list of the twenty key startup factors that you need to stridently address.

The Startup Landscape And Approach

According to the latest statistics, Venture Capital (VC) and Private Equity (PE) funds are flowing lavishly into budding startups that are striving to bring forth the latest and greatest in LegalTech, especially those newbie firms that are seeking to infuse state-of-the-art Artificial Intelligence (AI) into law practice legal systems and are aiming to demonstratively boost the day-to-day work of lawyers and other legal professionals.

There are quite a number of enterprising and spirited lawyers eyeing those LegalTech ventures and wondering whether they too have what it takes to launch into becoming an entrepreneur and take an outsized shot at making a go as a startup founder.

Here's how the entrepreneurial zeal typically gets rolling along.

Attorneys that are especially savvy when it comes to using computer-based legal systems can often readily discern what works for law offices and their fellow lawyers, and what does not work, along with ingeniously detecting the existence of gaps in coverage by the automation. This realization of an unmet need begins to fester inside their heads and becomes the spark to find a means of turning the seeming weakness or omission into an opportunity of bringing a new solution to the marketplace.

Okay, so the inspired lawyer knows the law and knows what lawyers do and ponders repeatedly how to make tech that will fill in the hole or otherwise bolster what other existing LegalTech cannot yet seem to accomplish.

Note that there is usually a wide chasm between the idea itself and the formulation of a software product that embodies that crafty idea.

Building robust software that can withstand the rigors of usage in law practices is not quite as easy as it might seem. Some of these budding entrepreneurs are overconfident about their programming skills, perhaps led to believe they have the needed software chops due to being a wizard with spreadsheets and handling legal databases with ease.

Be cautious in getting ahead of yourself.

Based on working with dozens of LegalTech firms and founders, you might want to seriously look before you leap into this, since the odds of such startups ultimately succeeding is dismally low, though admittedly the seasoning and experiences gained are apt to bolster your overall skills and make you into a stronger and more well-rounded attorney regardless of the entity outcome.

Generally, getting involved in or starting a new company is decidedly not for the faint of heart.

Keep in mind too that you should be cautious in betting the farm on that kind of jump. Sadly, some lawyers get so enamored about doing something new that they leave whatever paying job they have and falsely assume that they will soon be rolling in the dough from their new venture. More likely is that you will be devoting all your time and attention to the startup and won't be making a dime for quite some time.

You'll either need a cushy nest egg to keep you surviving or get a (rare) upfront bankroll to initially fund the effort. Even then, it is usually assumed that the key partners or founders will be putting skin into the game and the monies for the firm are supposed to go toward others such as software developers and non-legal staff that do your marketing or accounting.

One of the key tips is to put together a solid pitch deck that conveys what your startup is all about.

Notice that I said a pitch-deck and did not refer to a business plan.

It used to be that a lengthy strategic business plan was the recommended approach to depicting the vision of a new venture. These are still frequently put together, though the mainstay of attention goes toward a succinct pitch-deck instead (note, you can do both, rightfully so, namely having a detailed business plan and a corresponding pitch-deck that portrays the salient facets in a highly communicative manner).

If possible, you should also consider putting together a prototype of what you have in mind.

This is often crucial since it becomes a tangible means of showcasing what you hope to do.

A full-blown version of the prototype is normally referred to as a Minimally Viable Product (MVP) and provides enough of an indication of the proposed capability that you can do a demo, but it is also acceptable that the MVP lacks bells-and-whistles and is still a far cry from being ready for the real-world.

Twenty Factors That Make-Or-Break Your Startup

In any case, for your pitch-deck and a corresponding business plan, here are the essential twenty factors that you are expected to have considered:

1) Solvable Problem – what is the problem being solved and is it solvable in any practical way

2) Viable Solution – what is your proposed solution and is the solution feasible or not

3) Customers – what is your target market, its size, and its need for your proposed solution

4) This Is Similar To – what is your solution similar to, compare and contrast

5) Core Business Model – what is the business model that will underpin producing the solution

6) Product/Service – what is the nature of the product and/or the services involved

7) Differentiation – what makes this a Unique Value Proposition (UVP)

8) Startup Funding – what amount of startup funding and from which sources are you aiming

9) Monetization – what will ultimately be the ongoing sources of revenue and making money

10) Unfair Advantage – what do you have that provides a barrier to entry, such as IP

11) Your Expertise – what makes you suited for this kind of effort

12) Your Team – what team are you going to assemble and what talents are needed

13) Accomplished To-Date – what have you accomplished to-date on your startup quest

14) The Ask – what resources and monies do you need to get underway

15) Cost Structure – what are your anticipated costs and scalability facets

16) Exit Strategy – what are your end game goals and ideal exit

17) Marketing – what will be needed in terms of promotion, pricing, channels, etc.

18) Competitors – what are your competitors doing, including why they are missing the boat

19) Prior Pitches – what pitches have you been making and to whom, how did those go

20) The Pitch – what your pitch is will be judged as to whether you are investment-worthy

Admittedly, the list of those twenty factors seems daunting and nearly insurmountable, but they are actually all crucial to any startup worth its salt and require attention else the new venture is like a three-legged stool with one or more legs missing.

Being an entrepreneur can be exhilarating and the media loves to fawn over those that make it. You do not though often see the founders that regrettably floundered and were not able to get traction. There are lots and lots of those.

Undeniably, shifting from being a lawyer into becoming a flourishing entrepreneur has challenges, and each person needs to mindfully do some sober introspection about their situation and circumstances that either will propel them forward or bring their startup ambitions to a screeching halt.

Conclusion

Like any good attorney, make sure to study up and be sure that you have considered the favorable and disfavoring factors, and thoughtfully render a reasoned choice that proffers the best logic and highest chances for taking this moonshot-like breathtaking step.

Note: *For supplemental materials depicting the aspects discussed in this chapter, refer to Appendix B, which contains various augmented diagrams, charts, and additional related facets of relevance.*

CHAPTER 25

AI & LAW:
LEGALTECH PRODUCT IDEAS

Key briefing points about this essay:

- This is a continuation of an earlier article about the twenty key factors for a LegalTech startup

- In this piece, the focus is on two of the foundational factors: (1) the problem, (2) the solution

- If a LegalTech founder cannot clearly state the problem and proposed solution things will falter

- An example used herein discusses a startup proposing a contract life cycle management system

- Use these insights to ensure that your LegalTech startup has sharply devised its vision

Introduction

In Chapter 24, twenty overall key factors for LegalTech startups were introduced. Let's next take a close look at two of the factors, considered the most foundational and vital factors to first wrestle with:

- Identify a solvable problem

- Offer a viable solution

Believe it or not, those two key factors are oftentimes poorly stipulated by a startup founder and thusly renders the startup entirely suspect and unlikely to gain any traction.

Investors will not invest in a vacuous realm whereby the entrepreneur cannot distinctly and clearly state what the problem is and nor is the entrepreneur able to proffer what their proposed solution is. Likewise, rallying troops to your budding new ventures, such as attracting top-notch software engineers and other specialists will be problematic if you cannot definitively indicate the legal-realm problem and what the envisioned solution portends.

As a former top executive at a major Venture Capital (VC) firm, and now an angel investor that also serves as a pitch judge at various startup competitions, I routinely get pitched on LegalTech related new venture proposals that sadly miss the boat and fail to make abundantly clear what problem is being solved and how that problem can viably be solved.

This seemingly would be an obvious consideration to address, and it might be surprising to realize that many startup-focused lawyers do not somehow put those two factors at the forefront of their aims and aspirations. Instead, there is a tendency to concentrate on the structure of the new business, its cost model, its project revenues, and so on. The thing is if there is not a fundamental problem being solved by whatever the business is going to foster into the marketplace, the odds are that no one is going to ante up the dough to buy or subscribe to the product or service envisioned (and, likewise, few if any investors willing to put coinage into the endeavor).

Eye-Opening Example

Here's a quick example.

An eager and savvy attorney makes a pitch that a contract management system will be the basis for their startup venture and has already lined-up some ace programmers to write the code. Financial charts are shown with forecasted revenue that goes skyward.

It is tough to hold back from immediately asking pointed questions, torn between allowing the enthusiastic budding entrepreneur a chance to proffer their dream, and yet not wanting to waste time on something that might have minimal legs to stand on.

What's wrong with the new venture idea?

First, there is nothing stated about the problem being solved.

Sure, we can likely assume that a contract management system is going to solve some smattering of problems, but it is up to the entrepreneur to make that case. Presumably, the problem has to do with being more efficient or effective at handling, crafting, and fielding legal contracts, though this should not be a submerged aspect and ought to be at the top of the heap of reasons for the new venture to even exist.

What evidence exists to showcase that without the proposed solution, a contract management system, there is an outsized pain-point or stay-awake-at-night problem that needs to be solved?

In a sense, the cart has been placed in front of the horse, emphasizing the solution prior to clarifying and making the case that there is a problem that needs solving.

Let's assume that the attorney realizes the mishap and recovers by listing off a dozen solid reasons underlying today's mismanagement of contracts and how much wasted time and effort goes toward coping with legal contracts in a manual or paper-based mode.

Okay, you might say that there is now a notable problem in hand, including that there potentially is some form of solution to the articulated problem (side note: sometimes, a problem can be identified, but there is no reasonably solvable way to tackle it, such as saying that world hunger is the problem and for which there is not a likely practical solvable means for a startup to entirely "solve").

By establishing clarity about the problem, the next aspect to address is the proposed solution.

It is likely that for most problems there is a slew of possible solutions, out of which the attorney-to-entrepreneur has opted to choose some particular solution. Offering just one selected solution begs the question about what other solutions might exist and why none of those would be a better candidate for the new venture to concentrate on. If the entrepreneur has not considered other potential solutions, that's a red flag and suggests that they might get blindsided by something else that can solve the problem in a better way.

Also, if the proposed solution seems overly magical or unrealistic, this too can be a red flag.

Of course, there is also the consideration that the solution might already be in existence, and the attorney has failed to do their homework properly by figuring out how their solution will be able to eclipse those same solutions already being peddled.

In the case of a contract management system, I think we all already know that there is a boatload of such systems. The good news is that this suggests that indeed such systems are solving a known and accepted problem, else those systems would presumably not be selling and the firms providing them would go out of business.

The bad news is that unless the attorney-to-entrepreneur has some means to standout amongst the crowd and get their proposed contract management system to be sought over others, the me-too facets and competition by already entrenched entities will be the death knell for the fledgling startup.

Novelty Via Infusing AI

One path toward making a novel or innovative play in LegalTech involves infusing Artificial Intelligence (AI) into such systems. Potentially, the addition of AI could be a differentiator that makes a newly proposed LegalTech solution a possible game-changer.

Be cautious though in making outrageous claims of what AI will be able to achieve in your proposed solution. Admittedly, some make hyped assertions about AI and seem to get away with it, though one would anticipate that ultimately their ploys are bound to backfire and leave a tattered reputation in the trail of what might be a new venture disaster.

If an attorney is trying to brainstorm about what AI might bring to the table, it would behoove that outside-the-box thinking to make sure that you have knowledgeable advisers that know what is practical with AI, along with being able to see the trends coming down the pike in the next several years.

Another consideration is the chicken-or-the-egg conundrum.

The odds are that any AI addition is in fact additive, meaning that you need to have the underlying conventional LegalTech that serves underneath or aligned with the AI. Thus, continuing the contract management system example, a proposal to use AI such as Natural Language Processing (NLP) to readily allow legal teams to access and modify contracts is a relatively substantive benefit, as would be the use of Machine Learning (ML) to be able to piece together new contracts based on prior ones, but all of this capability presumes that a contracts database and access system underlies the AI facility.

In short, do you build the contract management system first, and then plop the AI on it, or do you craft the AI first and then look around to either augment an existing contract management system or opt to build one from scratch. It is the proverbial chicken-or-the-egg challenge.

The answer is that it depends on a variety of other factors and there is no single "right answer," such that it is up to the founder of the startup to indicate what approach they recommend and how they came to that pivotal recommendation. Sometimes it makes sense to derive the chicken first and then produce the egg, while in other instances the egg is devised first and the chicken arises thereafter.

In terms of the range of possibilities in LegalTech, take a reflective look at the work efforts in your law practice and those of your fellow legal professionals, and think introspectively about what automation might be able to do and how it could solve demonstratively thorny problems.

LegalTech Problem-Solution Product Spaces

As an exercise in LegalTech startup ideas formulation, I often list these kinds of tasks that arise in the practice of law, and use these to spark ideas for potential problems and viable solutions:

- Case Management
- Contracts
- Courts and Trials
- Discovery
- Documents/Records
- Intellectual Property (IP)
- Law Office
- Lawyer and Client Interaction
- Legal Assistants
- Legal Collaboration
- Legal Research
- Legal Workflow
- Legal Writing
- Professional Conduct
- Other

Conclusion

All told, in this brief exploration about getting your startup dreams into shape for the real world, keep in mind that you need to showcase clearly and succinctly the nature of the problem that you've singled out, along with making apparent why it is solvable, and then tie those facets to the vision of what a viable solution would look like.

This is a powerful one-two punch that will put your entrepreneurial spirit into gear and serve you well when aiming to get your new venture off the ground.

.

Note: *For supplemental materials depicting the aspects discussed in this chapter, refer to Appendix B, which contains various augmented diagrams, charts, and additional related facets of relevance.*

APPENDIX A

TEACHING WITH THIS MATERIAL
AND BIBLIOGRAPHY

The essays in this book can readily be used as a reading supplemental to augment traditional textbook-oriented content, particularly used in a class on AI or a class about the law.

Courses where this material is most likely applicable encompass classes at a college or university level.

Here are some typical settings that might apply:

o <u>Computer Science</u>. Classes studying AI, or possibly a CS social impacts class, etc.

o <u>Law</u>. Law classes exploring technology and its adoption for legal uses.

o <u>Sociology</u>. Sociology classes on the adoption and advancement of technology.

Specialized classes at the undergraduate and graduate level can also make use of this material.

For each chapter, consider whether you think the chapter provides material relevant to your course topic.

There are plenty of opportunities to get the students thinking about the topics and encourage them to decide whether they agree or disagree with the points offered and positions taken.

I would also encourage you to have the students do additional research beyond the chapter material presented (I provide next some suggested assignments that they can do).

RESEARCH ASSIGNMENTS ON THESE TOPICS

Your students can find research and background material on these topics, doing so in various tech journals, law journals, and other related publications.

Here are some suggestions for homework or projects that you could assign to students:

a) <u>Assignment for foundational AI research topics</u>: Research and prepare a paper and a presentation on a specific aspect of AI, such as Machine Learning, ANN, etc. The paper should cite at least 3 reputable sources. Compare and contrast to what has been stated in the chosen chapter.

b) <u>Assignment for Law topics</u>: Research and prepare a paper covering Law aspects via at least 3 reputable sources and analyze the characterizations. Compare and contrast to what has been stated in the chosen chapter.

c) <u>Assignment for a Business topic</u>: Research and prepare a paper and a presentation on businesses and advanced technology regarding AI and Law. What is trending, and why? Make sure to cite at least 3 reputable sources. Compare and contrast to the depictions herein.

d) <u>Assignment to do a Startup:</u> Have the students prepare a paper or business plan about how they might start up a business in this realm. They could also be asked to present their business plan and should also have a prepared presentation deck to coincide with it.

You can certainly adjust the aforementioned assignments to fit your particular needs and class structure.

You'll notice that I usually suggest that (at least) 3 reputable cited sources be utilized for the paper writing-based assignments.

I usually steer students toward "reputable" publications, since otherwise, they will cite some less reliable sources that have little or no credentials, other than that they happened to appear online was easy to retrieve. You can, of course, define "reputable" in whatever way you prefer, for example, some faculty think Wikipedia is not reputable while others believe it is reputable and allow students to cite it.

The reason that I usually ask for at least 3 citations is that if the student only relies upon one or two citations, they usually settle on whatever they happened to find the fastest. By requiring 3 (or more) citations, it usually seems to inspire them to explore more extensively and likely end-up finding five or more sources, and then whittling it down to 3 if so needed.

I have not specified the length of their papers and leave that to you to tell the students what you prefer.

For each of those assignments, you could end up with a short one to two-pager or you could do a dissertation length in-depth paper. Base the length on whatever best fits for your class, and likewise the credit amount of the assignment within the context of the other grading metrics you'll be using for the class.

I usually try to get students to present their work, in addition to doing the writing. This is a helpful practice for what they will do in the business world. Most of the time, they will be required to prepare an analysis and present it. If you don't have the class time or inclination to have the students present their papers, then you can presumably omit the aspect of them putting together presentations.

GUIDE TO USING THE CHAPTERS

For each of the chapters, I provide the next some various ways to use the chapter contents.

You can assign the below tasks as individual homework assignments, or the tasks can be used for team projects. You can easily layout a series of assignments, such as indicating that the students are to do item "a" below for say Chapter 1, then "b" for the next chapter of the book, and so on.

a) What is the main point of the chapter and describe in your own words the significance of the topic.

b) Identify at least two aspects in the chapter that you agree with and support your concurrence by providing at least one other outside researched item as support; make sure to explain your basis for agreeing with the aspects.

c) Identify at least two aspects in the chapter that you disagree with and support your disagreement by providing at least one other outside researched item as support; make sure to explain your basis for disagreeing with the aspects.

d) Find an aspect that was not covered extensively in the chapter, doing so by conducting outside research, and then offer an expanded indication about how that aspect ties into the chapter, along with the added significance it brings to the topic.

e) Interview a specialist in the industry about the topic of the chapter, collect from them their thoughts and opinions, and readdress the chapter by citing your source and how they compared and contrasted to the material,

f) Interview a relevant professor or researcher in a college or university setting about the topic of the chapter, collect from them their thoughts and opinions, and readdress the chapter by citing your source and how they compared and contrasted to the material,

g) Try to update a chapter by finding out the latest on the topic and ascertain whether the issue or topic has now been solved or whether it is still being addressed, explain what you come up with.

The above are all ways in which you can get the students of your class involved in considering the material of a given chapter. You could mix things up by having one of those above assignments per each week, covering the chapters over the course of the semester or quarter.

SUGGESTED REFERENCES TO EXPLORE

To help get your students started in finding relevant and important papers on the topic of AI and the law, I provide next a handy bibliography that can be utilized.

You could also assign the students to each (or in teams) read an assigned reference from the list, and then have them provide either a written summary and review or do so as part of a classroom presentation.

BIBLIOGRAPHIC REFERENCES

1. Aleven, Vincent (1997). "Teaching Case-Based Argumentation Through a Model and Examples," Ph.D. Dissertation, University of Pittsburgh.

2. Aleven, Vincent (2003). "Using Background Knowledge in Case-Based Legal Reasoning: A Computational Model and an Intelligent Learning Environment," Artificial Intelligence.

3. Amgoud, Leila (2012). "Five Weaknesses of ASPIC+," Volume 299, Communications in Computer and Information Science (CCIS).

4. Antonious, Grigoris, and George Baryannis, Sotiris Batsakis, Guido Governatori, Livio Robaldo, Givoanni Siragusa, Ilias Tachmazidis (2018). "Legal Reasoning and Big Data: Opportunities and Challenges," August 2018, MIREL Workshop on Mining and Reasoning Legal Texts.

5. Ashley, Kevin (1991). "Reasoning with Cases and Hypotheticals in HYPO," Volume 34, International Journal of Man-Machine Studies.

6. Ashley, Kevin, and Karl Branting, Howard Margolis, and Cass Sunstein (2001). "Legal Reasoning and Artificial Intelligence: How Computers 'Think' Like Lawyers," Symposium: Legal Reasoning and Artificial Intelligence, University of Chicago Law School Roundtable.

7. Baker, Jamie (2018). "A Legal Research Odyssey: Artificial Intelligence as Disrupter," Law Library Journal.

8. Batsakis, Sotiris, and George Baryannis, Guido Governatori, Illias Tachmazidis, Grigoris Antoniou (2018). "Legal Representation and Reasoning in Practice: A Critical Comparison," Volume 313, Legal Knowledge and Information Systems.

9. Bench-Capon, Trevor (2004). "AGATHA: Automation of the Construction of Theories in Case Law Domains," January 2004, Legal Knowledge and Information Systems Jurix 2004, Amsterdam.

10. Bench-Capon, Trevor (2012). "Representing Popov v Hayashi with Dimensions and Factors," March 2012, Artificial Intelligence and Law.

11. Bench-Capon, Trevor, and Givoanni Sartor (2003). "A Model of Legal Reasoning with Cases Incorporating Theories and Values," November 2013, Artificial Intelligence.

12. Breuker, Joost (1996). "A Functional Ontology of Law," October 1996, ResearchGate.

13. Bruninghaus, Stefanie, and Kevin Ashley (2003). "Combining Case-Based and Model-Based Reasoning for Predicting the Outcome of Legal Cases," June 2003, ICCBR'03: Proceedings of the 5th International Conference on Case-based reasoning: Research and Development.

14. Buchanan, Bruce, and Thomas Headrick (1970). "Some Speculation about Artificial Intelligence and Legal Reasoning," Volume 23, Stanford Law Review.

15. Chagal-Feferkorn, Karni (2019). "Am I An Algorithm or a Product: When Products Liability Should Apply to Algorithmic Decision-Makers," Stanford Law & Policy Review.

16. Douglas, William (1948). "The Dissent: A Safeguard of Democracy," Volume 32, Journal of the American Judicature Society.

17. Dung, P, and R. Kowalski, F. Toni (2006). "Dialectic Proof Procedures for Assumption-Based Admissible Argumentation," Artificial Intelligence.

18. Eliot, Lance (2020). AI And Legal Reasoning Essentials. LBE Press Publishing.

19. Eliot, Lance (2020). Artificial Intelligence and LegalTech Essentials. LBE Press Publishing.

20. Eliot, Lance (2020). "FutureLaw 2020 Showcases How Tech is Transforming The Law, Including the Impacts of AI," April 16, 2020, Forbes.

21. Erdem, Esra, and Michael Gelfond, Nicola Leone (2016). "Applications of Answer Set Programming," AI Magazine.

22. Gardner, Anne (1987). Artificial Intelligence and Legal Reasoning. MIT Press.

23. Genesereth, Michael (2009). "Computational Law: The Cop in the Backseat," Stanford Center for Legal Informatics, Stanford University.

24. Ghosh, Mirna (2019). "Automation of Legal Reasoning and Decision Based on Ontologies," Normandie Universite.

25. Grabmair, Matthias (2017). "Predicting Trade Secret Case Outcomes using Argument Schemes and Learned Quantitative Value Effect Tradeoffs," IJCAI June 12, 2017, London, United Kingdom.

26. Hage, Jaap (1996). "A Theory of Legal Reasoning and a Logic to Match," Volume 4, Artificial Intelligence and Law.

27. Hage, Jaap (2000). "Dialectical Models in Artificial Intelligence and Law," Artificial Intelligence and Law.

28. Hage, Japp, and Ronald Leenes, Arno Lodder (1993). "Hard Cases: A Procedural Approach," Artificial Intelligence and Law.

29. Hobbes, Thomas (1651). The Matter, Form, and Power of a Common-Wealth Ecclesiasticall and Civil.

30. Holmes, Oliver (1897). "The Path of the Law," Volume 10, Harvard Law Review.

31. Katz, Daniel, and Michael Bommarito, Josh Blackman (2017). "A General Approach for Predicting the Behavior of the Supreme Court of the United States," April 12, 2017, PLOS ONE.

32. Kowalski, Robert, and Francesca Toni (1996). "Abstract Argumentation," AI-Law96.

33. Laswell, Harold (1955). "Current Studies of the Decision Process: Automation Creativity," Volume 8, Western Political Quarterly.

34. Libal, Tomer, and Alexander Steen (2019). "The NAI Suite: Drafting and Reasoning over Legal Texts," October 15, 2019, arXiv.

35. Lipton, Zachary (2017). "The Mythos of Model Interpretability," March 6, 2017, arXiv.

36. Martin, Andrew, and Kevin Quinn, Theodore Ruger, Pauline Kim (2004). "Competing Approaches to Predicting Supreme Court Decision Making," December 2014, Symposium on Forecasting U.S. Supreme Court Decisions.

37. McCarty, Thorne (1977). "Reflections on TAXMAN: An Experiment in Artificial Intelligence and Legal Reasoning," January 1977, Harvard Law Review.

38. Modgil, Sanjay, and Henry Prakken (2013). "The ASPIC+ Framework for Structured Argumentation: A Tutorial," December 16, 2013, Argument & Computation.

39. Mowbray, Andrew, and Philip Chung, Graham Greenleaf (2019). "Utilising AI in the Legal Assistance Sector," LegalAIIA Workshop, ICAIL, June 17, 2019, Montreal, Canada.

40. Parasuraman, Raja, and Thomas Sheridan, Christopher Wickens (2000). "A Model for Types and Levels of Human Interaction with Automation," May 2000, IEEE Transactions on Systems, Man, and Cybernetics.

41. Popple, James (1993). "SHYSTER: A Pragmatic Legal Expert System," Ph.D. Dissertation, Australian National University.

42. Prakken, Henry, and Giovanni Sartor (2015). "Law and Logic: A Review from an Argumentation Perspective," Volume 227, Artificial Intelligence.

43. Rissland, Edwina (1988). Artificial Intelligence and Legal Reasoning: A Discussion of the Field and Gardner's Book," Volume 9, AI Magazine.

44. Rissland, Edwina (1990). "Artificial Intelligence and Law: Stepping Stones to a Model of Legal Reasoning," Yale Law Journal.

45. Searle, John (1980). "Minds, Brains, and Programs," Volume 3, Behavioral and Brain Sciences.

46. Sunstein, Cass (2001). "Of Artificial Intelligence and Legal Reasoning," University of Chicago Law School, Public Law and Legal Theory Working Papers.

47. Sunstein, Cass, and Kevin Ashley, Karl Branting, Howard Margolis (2001). "Legal Reasoning and Artificial Intelligence: How Computers 'Think' Like Lawyers," Symposium: Legal Reasoning and Artificial Intelligence, University of Chicago Law School Roundtable.

48. Surden, Harry (2014). "Machine Learning and Law," Washington Law Review.

49. Surden, Harry (2019). "Artificial Intelligence and Law: An Overview," Summer 2019, Georgia State University Law Review.

50. Valente, Andre, and Joost Breuker (1996). "A Functional Ontology of Law," Artificial Intelligence and Law.

51. Waltl, Bernhard, and Roland Vogl (2018). "Explainable Artificial Intelligence: The New Frontier in Legal Informatics," February 2018, Jusletter IT 22, Stanford Center for Legal Informatics, Stanford University.

52. Wittgenstein, Ludwig (1953). Philosophical Investigations. Blackwell Publishing.

APPENDIX B
SUPPLEMENTAL
FIGURES AND CHARTS

For the convenience of viewing, supplemental figures and charts
related to the topics discussed are shown on the next pages

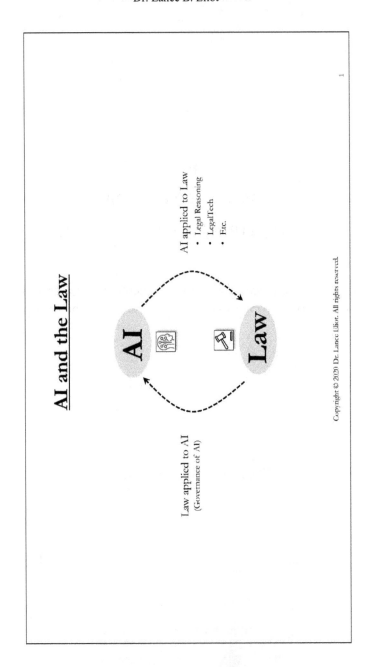

Figure 1

AI & Law: Levels of Autonomy For AI Legal Reasoning (AILR)

Level	Descriptor	Examples	Automation	Status
0	No Automation	Manual, paper-based (no automation)	None	De Facto - In Use
1	Simple Assistance Automation	Word Processing, XLS, online legal docs, etc.	Legal Assist	Widely In Use
2	Advanced Assistance Automation	Query-style NLP, ML for case prediction, etc.	Legal Assist	Some In Use
3	Semi-Autonomous Automation	KBS & ML/DL for legal reasoning & analysis, etc.	Legal Assist	Primarily Prototypes & Research Based
4	AILR Domain Autonomous	Versed only in a specific legal domain	Legal Advisor (law fluent)	None As Yet
5	AILR Fully Autonomous	Versatile within and across all legal domains	Legal Advisor (law fluent)	None As Yet
6	AILR Superhuman Autonomous	Exceeds human-based legal reasoning	Supra Legal Advisor	Indeterminate

v1.3

Source Author: Dr. Lance B. Eliot

Figure 1: AI & Law - Autonomous Levels by Rows

Figure 2

AI & Law: Levels of Autonomy For AI Legal Reasoning (AILR)

	Level 0	Level 1	Level 2	Level 3	Level 4	Level 5	Level 6
Descriptor	No Automation	Simple Assistance Automation	Advanced Assistance Automation	Semi-Autonomous Automation	AILR Domain Autonomous	AILR Fully Autonomous	AILR Superhuman Autonomous
Examples	Manual, paper-based (no automation)	Word Processing, XLS, online legal docs, etc.	Query-style NLP, ML for case prediction, etc.	KBS & ML/DL for legal reasoning & analysis, etc.	Versed only in a specific legal domain	Versatile within and across all legal domains	Exceeds human-based legal reasoning
Automation	None	Legal Assist	Legal Assist	Legal Assist	Legal Advisor (law fluent)	Legal Advisor (law fluent)	Supra Legal Advisor
Status	De Facto – In Use	Widely In Use	Some In Use	Primarily Prototypes & Research-based	None As Yet	None As Yet	Indeterminate

v1.3

Figure 2: AI & Law - Autonomous Levels by Columns   *Source Author: Dr. Lance B. Eliot*

Figure 3

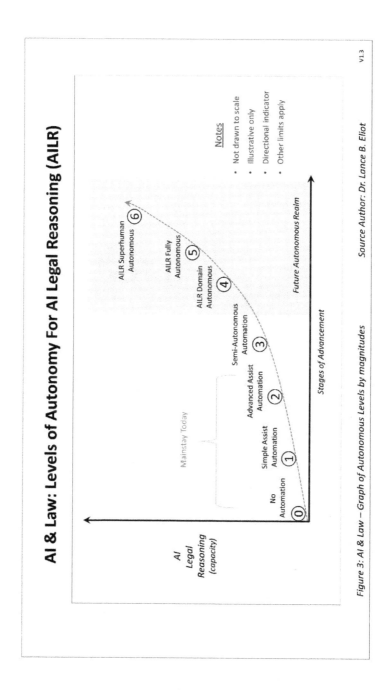

Figure 4

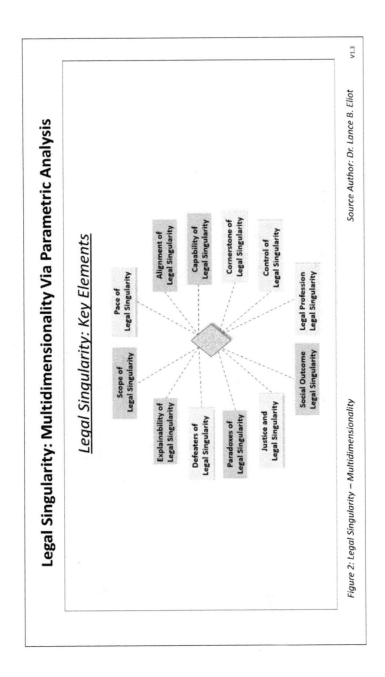

Figure 5

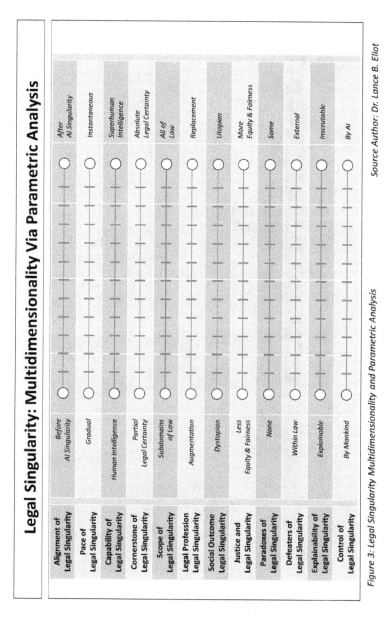

Figure 3: Legal Singularity Multidimensionality and Parametric Analysis

Source Author: Dr. Lance B. Eliot

Figure 6

Legal Micro-Directives: Levels of Autonomy For AI Legal Reasoning (AILR)

	Level 0	Level 1	Level 2	Level 3	Level 4	Level 5	Level 6
Descriptor	No Automation	Simple Assistance Automation	Advanced Assistance Automation	Semi-Autonomous Automation	AILR Domain Autonomous	AILR Fully Autonomous	AILR Superhuman Autonomous
Examples	Manual, paper-based (no automation)	Word Processing, XLS, online legal docs, etc.	Query-style NLP, ML for case prediction, etc.	KBS & ML/DL for legal reasoning & analysis, etc.	Versed only in a specific legal domain	Versatile within and across all legal domains	Exceeds human-based legal reasoning
Automation	None	Legal Assist	Legal Assist	Legal Assist	Legal Advisor (law fluent)	Legal Advisor (law fluent)	Supra Legal Advisor
Status	De Facto – In Use	Widely In Use	Some In Use	Primarily Prototypes & Research-based	None As Yet	None As Yet	Indeterminate
AI-Enabled Legal Micro-Directives	*n/a*	*Impractical*	*Incubatory*	*Infancy*	*Narrow*	*Wide*	*Consummate*

v1.3

Figure 1: Legal Micro-Directives - Autonomous Levels of AILR by Columns

Source Author: Dr. Lance B. Eliot

Figure 7

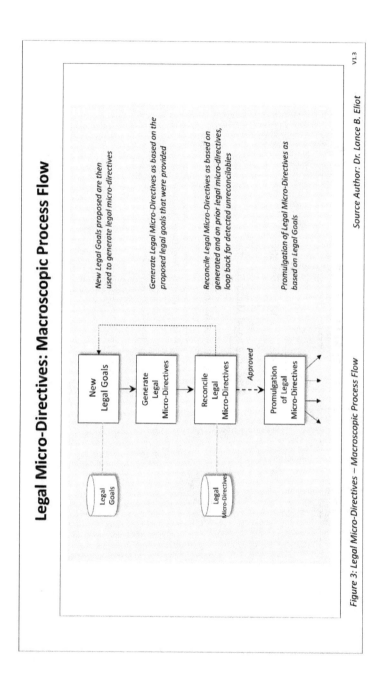

Figure 8

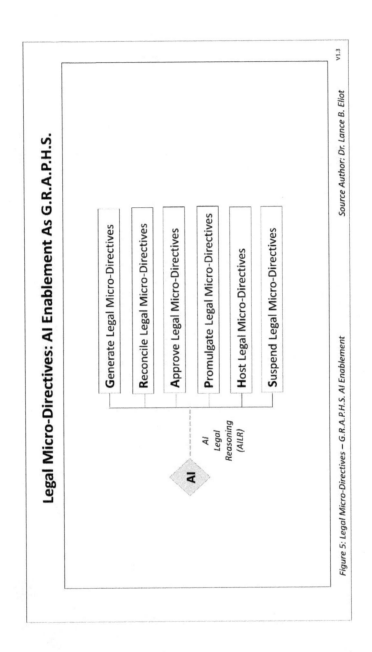

Figure 5: Legal Micro-Directives – G.R.A.P.H.S. AI Enablement

Figure 9

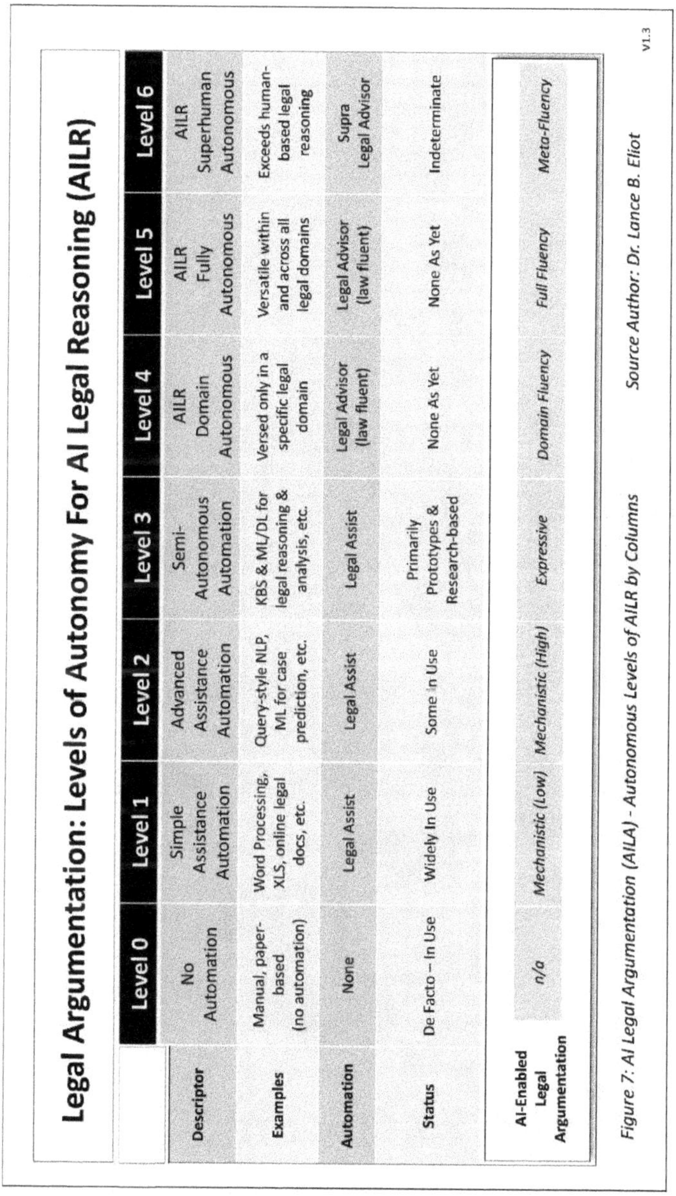

Legal Argumentation: Levels of Autonomy For AI Legal Reasoning (AILR)

	Level 0	Level 1	Level 2	Level 3	Level 4	Level 5	Level 6
Descriptor	No Automation	Simple Assistance Automation	Advanced Assistance Automation	Semi-Autonomous Automation	AILR Domain Autonomous	AILR Fully Autonomous	AILR Superhuman Autonomous
Examples	Manual, paper-based (no automation)	Word Processing, XLS, online legal docs, etc.	Query-style NLP, ML for case prediction, etc.	KBS & ML/DL for legal reasoning & analysis, etc.	Versed only in a specific legal domain	Versatile within and across all legal domains	Exceeds human-based legal reasoning
Automation	None	Legal Assist	Legal Assist	Legal Assist	Legal Advisor (law fluent)	Legal Advisor (law fluent)	Supra Legal Advisor
Status	De Facto – In Use	Widely In Use	Some in Use	Primarily Prototypes & Research-based	None As Yet	None As Yet	Indeterminate
AI-Enabled Legal Argumentation	n/a	Mechanistic (Low)	Mechanistic (High)	Expressive	Domain Fluency	Full Fluency	Meta-Fluency

v1.3

Figure 7: AI Legal Argumentation (AILA) - Autonomous Levels of AILR by Columns   Source Author: Dr. Lance B. Eliot

Figure 10

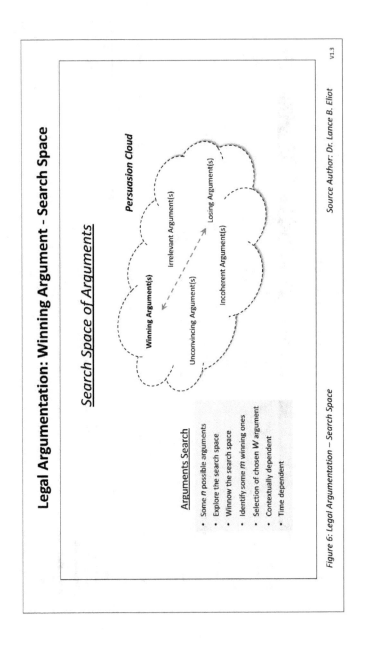

Figure 11

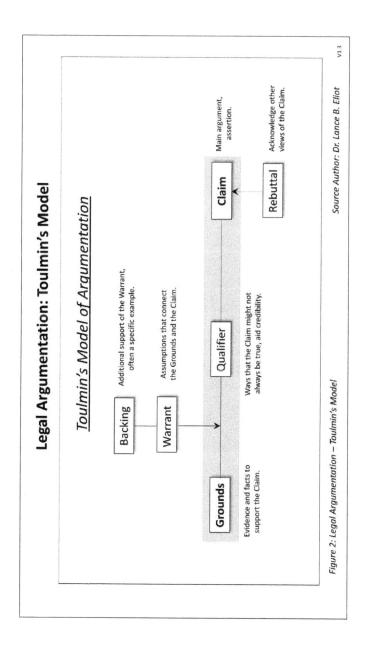

Figure 12

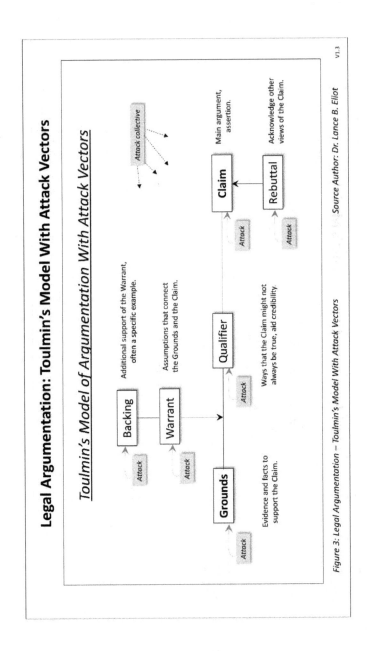

Figure 13

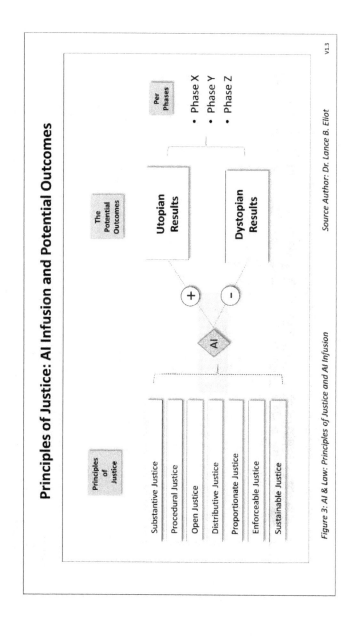

Figure 14

Principles of Justice and Autonomous Levels of AI Legal Reasoning (AILR)

Descriptor	Level 0 No Automation	Level 1 Simple Assistance Automation	Level 2 Advanced Assistance Automation	Level 3 Semi-Autonomous Automation	Level 4 AILR Domain Autonomous	Level 5 AILR Fully Autonomous	Level 6 AILR Superhuman Autonomous
Substantive Justice	Traditional	Traditional	Traditional	Emerging	Phase X Impacts	Phase Y Impacts	Phase Z Impacts
Procedural Justice	Traditional	Traditional	Traditional	Emerging	Phase X Impacts	Phase Y Impacts	Phase Z Impacts
Open Justice	Traditional	Traditional	Traditional	Emerging	Phase X Impacts	Phase Y Impacts	Phase Z Impacts
Distributive Justice	Traditional	Traditional	Traditional	Emerging	Phase X Impacts	Phase Y Impacts	Phase Z Impacts
Proportionate Justice	Traditional	Traditional	Traditional	Emerging	Phase X Impacts	Phase Y Impacts	Phase Z Impacts
Enforceable Justice	Traditional	Traditional	Traditional	Emerging	Phase X Impacts	Phase Y Impacts	Phase Z Impacts
Sustainable Justice	Traditional	Traditional	Traditional	Emerging	Phase X Impacts	Phase Y Impacts	Phase Z Impacts

v1.3

Source Author: Dr. Lance B. Eliot

Figure 1: AI & Law – Principles of Justice and LoA AILR by Columns

Figure 15

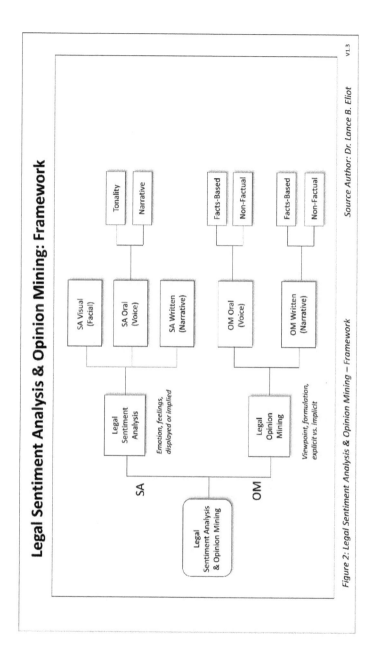

Figure 16

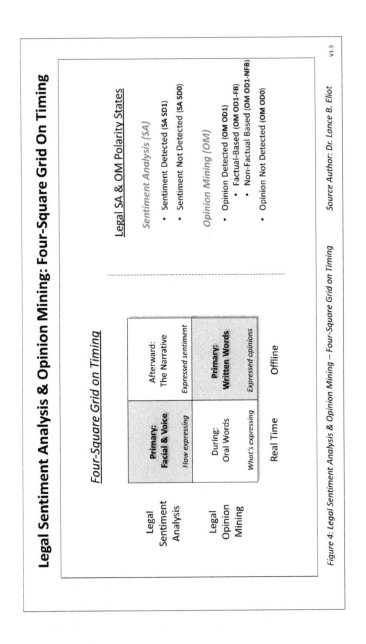

Figure 4: Legal Sentiment Analysis & Opinion Mining – Four-Square Grid on Timing   Source Author: Dr. Lance B. Eliot

Figure 17

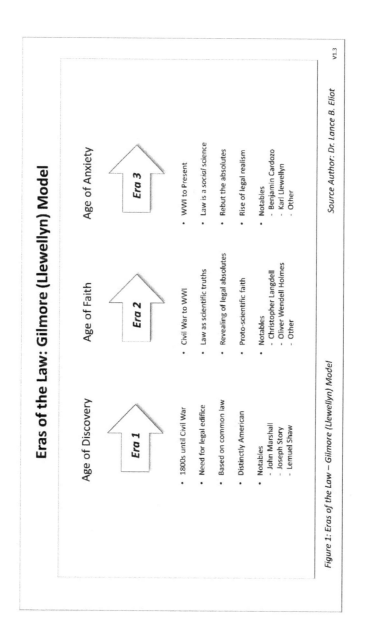

Figure 1: Eras of the Law – Gilmore (Llewellyn) Model

Figure 18

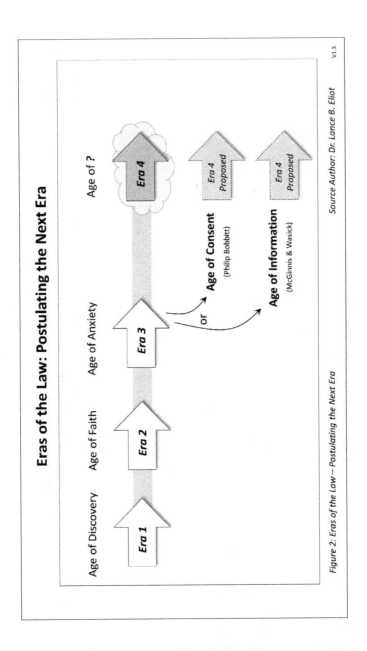

Figure 19

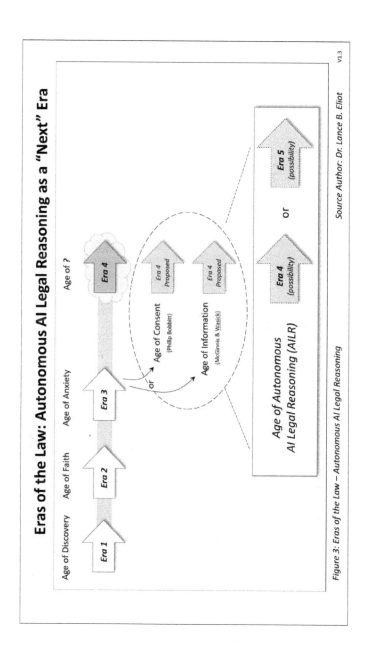

Figure 20

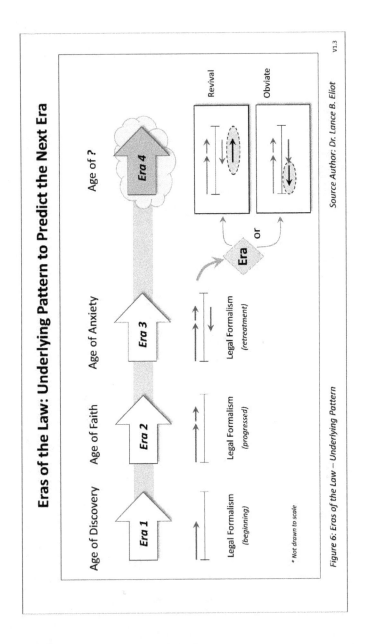

Figure 21

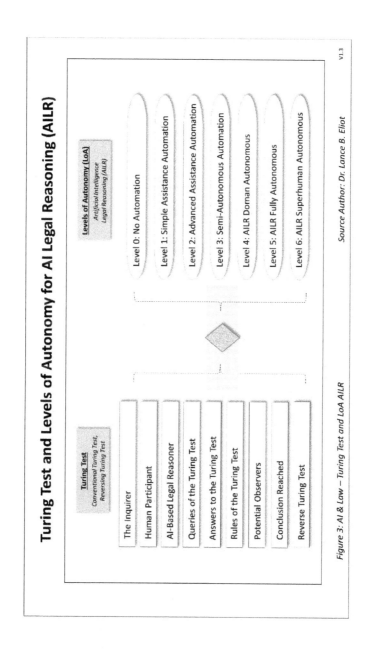

Figure 22

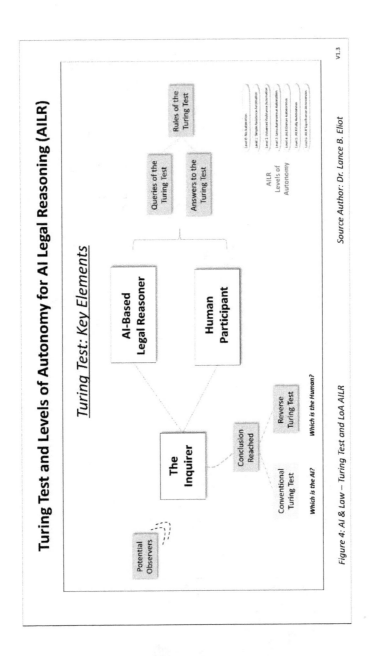

Figure 23

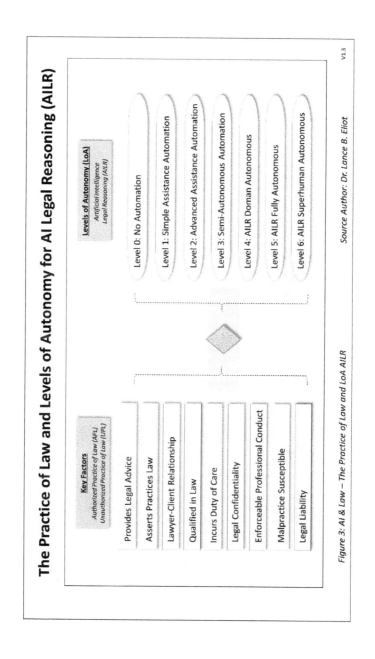

Figure 24

The Practice of Law and Autonomous Levels of AI Legal Reasoning (AILR)

V1.3

Descriptor	Level 0 No Automation	Level 1 Simple Assistance Automation	Level 2 Advanced Assistance Automation	Level 3 Semi-Autonomous Automation	Level 4 AILR Domain Autonomous	Level 5 AILR Fully Autonomous	Level 6 AILR Superhuman Autonomous
Provides Legal Advice	n/a	No	Maybe	Yes	Yes	Yes	Yes Plus
Asserts Practices Law	n/a	No	No	No	Yes	Yes	Yes Plus
Lawyer–Client Relationship	n/a	No	No	No	Partial	Yes	Yes
Qualified in Law	n/a	No	No	Minimal	Partial	Yes	Yes Plus
Incurs Duty of Care	n/a	No	No	No	Likely	Yes	Yes
Legal Confidentiality	n/a	No	No	No	Likely	Yes	Yes
Enforceable Prof Conduct	n/a	No	No	No	Likely	Yes	Yes
Malpractice Susceptible	n/a	No	No	No	Likely	Yes	Yes
Legal Liability	n/a	No	Maybe	Likely	Likely	Yes	Yes

Strawman Variant

Figure 1: AI & Law – The Practice of Law and LoA AILR by Columns

Source Author: Dr. Lance B. Eliot

Figure 25

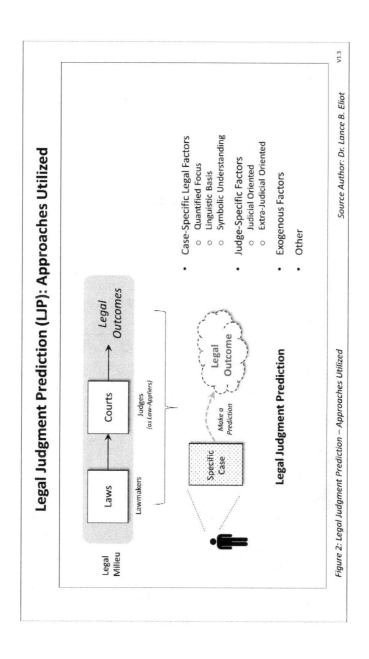

Figure 26

233

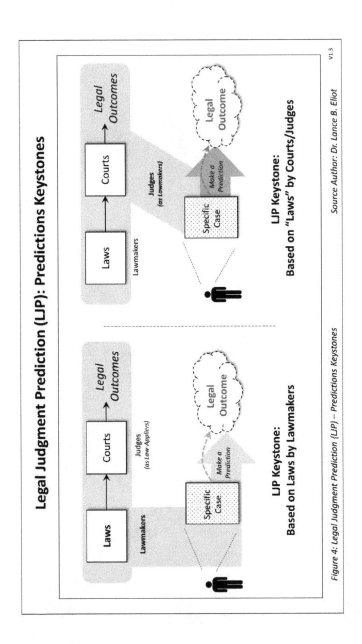

Figure 4: Legal Judgment Prediction (LJP) – Predictions Keystones

Figure 27

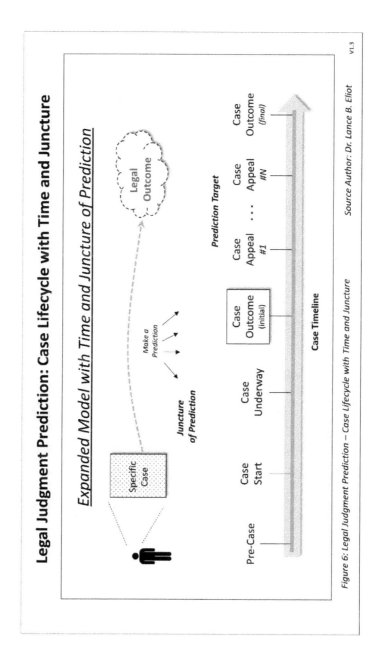

Figure 6: Legal Judgment Prediction – Case Lifecycle with Time and Juncture

Figure 28

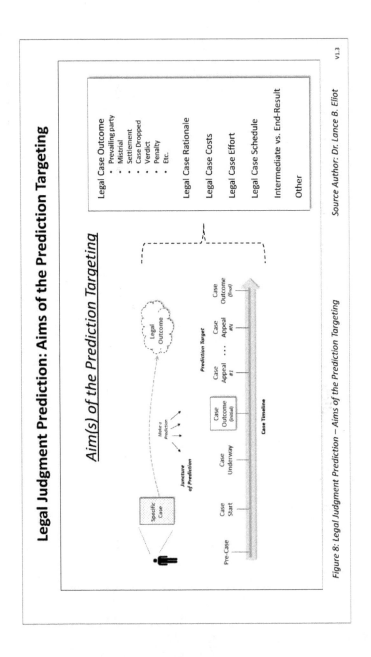

Figure 8: Legal Judgment Prediction – Aims of the Prediction Targeting

Figure 29

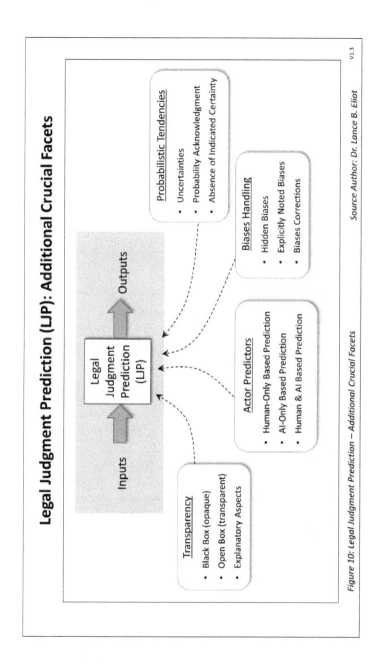

Figure 10: Legal Judgment Prediction – Additional Crucial Facets

Figure 30

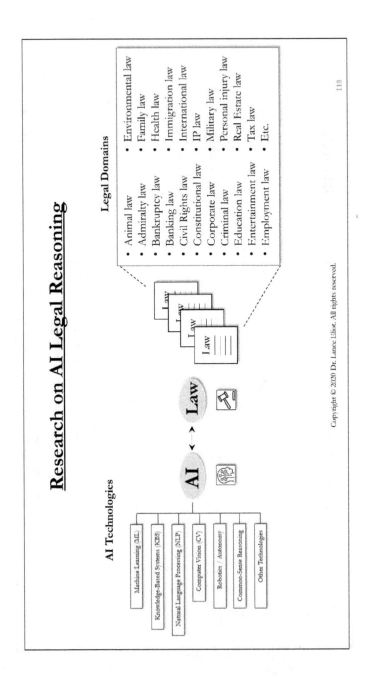

Figure 31

ABOUT THE AUTHOR

Dr. Lance B. Eliot, Ph.D., MBA is a globally recognized AI expert and thought leader, an invited Stanford Fellow at Stanford University, an experienced top executive and corporate leader, a successful entrepreneur, and a noted scholar on AI, including that his Forbes and AI Trends columns have amassed over 4 million views, his books on AI are ranked in the Top 10 of all-time AI books, his journal articles are widely cited, and he has developed and implemented numerous AI systems.

He currently serves as the Chief AI Scientist at Techbruim, Inc. and has over twenty years of industry experience including serving as a corporate officer in billion-dollar sized firms and was a partner in a major consulting firm. He is also a successful entrepreneur having founded, ran, and sold several high-tech related businesses.

Dr. Eliot previously hosted the popular radio show *Technotrends* that was also available on American Airlines flights via their in-flight audio program, he has made appearances on CNN, has been a frequent speaker at industry conferences, and his podcasts have been downloaded over 150,000 times.

A former professor at the University of Southern California (USC), he founded and led an innovative research lab on Artificial Intelligence. He also previously served on the faculty of the University of California Los Angeles (UCLA) and was a visiting professor at other major universities. He was elected to the International Board of the Society for Information Management (SIM), a prestigious association of over 3,000 high-tech executives worldwide.

He has performed extensive community service, including serving as Senior Science Adviser to the Congressional Vice-Chair of the Congressional Committee on Science & Technology. He has served on the Board of the OC Science & Engineering Fair (OCSEF), where he is also has been a Grand Sweepstakes judge, and likewise served as a judge for the Intel International SEF (ISEF). He served as the Vice-Chair of the Association for Computing Machinery (ACM) Chapter, a prestigious association of computer scientists. Dr. Eliot has been a shark tank judge for the USC Mark Stevens Center for Innovation on start-up pitch competitions and served as a mentor for several incubators and accelerators in Silicon Valley and in Silicon Beach.

Dr. Eliot holds a Ph.D. from USC, MBA, and Bachelor's in Computer Science, and earned the CDP, CCP, CSP, CDE, and CISA certifications

ADDENDUM

Thanks for reading this book and I hope you will continue your interest in the field of AI & Law

---

For my free podcasts about AI & Law:

https://ai-law.libsyn.com/website

Those podcasts are also available on Spotify, iTunes, etc.

For the latest on AI & Law see my website:

www.ai-law.legal

To follow me on Twitter:

https://twitter.com/LanceEliot

For my in-depth book on AI & Law:

AI And Legal Reasoning Essentials

www.amazon.com/gp/product/1734601655/